Burn Your Couch

A Manifesto for the Average Averse

Dedication

This book is dedicated to Tyler Trahan, who, at the far-too-young age of twenty-two, selflessly gave his life in service to the United States of America on April 30, 2009, during Operation Iraqi Freedom. Tyler was a man who always knew exactly what he wanted while sporting a character unswayable by anything this world could present.

He died doing what he believed in and lived doing what he loved. I'm one of many who are a better human simply for having known him, and by that virtue, the world is better because for a brief period, he was part of it. Like so many others who have found themselves exposed to the harsh brutalities of war, his family has had to shoulder more burden than is humane and more grief than is manageable. To them, I find myself humbled in gratitude. I am only able to write this book and do what I love today because you and people like you had the strength to raise a hero. From the bottom of my heart, thank you.

Table of Contents

Prologue. Commonplace Growth

"Life is born of struggle and striving, and true joy and understanding do not come from comfort and safety; they come from epiphany born in exhaustion. Safety and comfort are mortal danger to the soul."
—Sam Sheridan, A Fighter's Heart

It's two o'clock in the afternoon, and the North Carolina sun is exactly what I need. I've been running for nine and a half hours, and the pain behind my right knee comes and goes. It seems a bit duller than usual at the moment, so I'm assuming my pain receptors have quit trying to make me stop moving. The electrolytes and sodium from the chicken soup and a fistful of gummy bears at the last aid station must be digesting well because, for the first time in what feels like hours, I'm conscious of something other than how badly I want to lie down on the side of the road and fall asleep, preferably to wake up in a world where running for four more hours isn't part of my future. For once, though, I feel free. For the first time in a long time, I feel free to breathe in this beautiful seventy-five-degree day and appreciate the world from a different point of view, one that can only be seen through the appreciation of time spent making progress under my own power. Mostly though, because I recognize that a large part of the pain is finally in my rearview mirror, I feel free to believe that I can, for now, conquer whatever lies ahead of me. Ahh, runner's high is a good thing.

So many things become clear when one is three-quarters of the way through a fifty-four-mile foot race. A quick disclaimer: at the time of this race, I did not yet consider myself in any way a runner. In fact, before this race, the longest I had run at any single time in the previous year was between one and three miles. I had just returned from a deployment overseas with the military, and considerably more time spent in the gym had left me about twenty-five pounds heavier than the last time I had run any kind of distance. But I ascribe to the notion that human beings do not grow as individuals without being challenged. The consistency of comfort has always rubbed me the wrong way if I do not at least try to push back against it.

Fast forward to five o'clock in the evening, and I have finally gotten to that breakthrough aha moment. Questions that I usually could not answer could now be explained. As you can imagine, leading up to the race, I faced no lack of questioning from friends and family, who had begun to wonder aloud if I was possibly losing my mind for good. Plenty of times during the race, that same question ran through my own mind. *Why put yourself through this? Why so soon? Why not pick one so that you have enough time to train for it? What do you have to prove? Who are you trying to impress?*

I couldn't answer these questions until five o'clock while in the euphoria of being decently close to completing the hardest physical thing that I had done outside of the military. I was proving nothing to anyone except myself. I was conquering a goal because I found an incredible amount of empowerment in knowing that I could. I wasn't out there to beat anyone else. I was out there to break through physical and mental barriers I had personally come up against. I was running because I have always felt a certain responsibility to myself to settle for nothing but constant improvement, which I have had to accept, is only found through constant challenge. This particular battle with gravity taught me a lesson about life that I will take with me and apply to everything I do until the day I die; If I am willing to put in the work, great salvation can be found in the depths of suffering. And that is the answer to the most common question I got leading up to these twelve-plus hours of running, which was, "Do you like the pain"?

Contrary to what many people think, I don't love pain. Actually, I don't even like it. I just see it as a necessary evil. What I love is the window that pain creates and the opportunity it provides. Experiencing pain provides an unbiased look deep into the soul of the person who is suffering and serves as an undeniable litmus test for those who long to know what they are made of and how deep their resolve runs. Enduring pain provides deliverance because, at some point, deep in the trenches, further than most people are willing to go, the sufferer realizes that pain is inviting them to life's proving grounds. True pain will leave nowhere to hide and no way of escape except to face it and move through it. This process is what forces the mental fortitude I seek in an event like this. There is no easier way. Like so many stoics have understood, the answer isn't found by going around. You must go through.

Structure of the book

A commonplace book or "commonplaces," as they were referred to in early modern Europe where they began gaining significance, is a way to compile knowledge. They are scrapbooks filled with items of every kind, from recipes to thoughts, prayers, poems, ideas, whatever the owner finds relevant and worth remembering. While typically used by scholars, writers, and students to remember significant concepts that they have learned, anyone can benefit from such a practice. Not only is it useful to the keeper of the book, but it also makes a great gift for someone else. Your life is filled with adventure, risk, drama, lessons, and growth; why not document it so others can learn from all you have been through?

I have personally struggled for years to get all these thoughts down in a single linear fashion so they could be easily understood by other people. This book is a collection of thoughts, concepts, and notions that have proven useful to my personal growth. They are not necessarily connected in a linear story. Some, I have pulled from business lessons, some have been taken from my pursuit of health and fitness, and some have been pulled from my military experience, a venture that took up a decade of my life and gave me much of the opportunity that I am thankful for today.

The truth is, I am not sure anyone will want to read this book. Art always seems to walk a strikingly thin line between interesting people and not, and I have no idea what side of that line this book will fall on. Either way, I needed to write it. The lessons from my life experience demanded it. On some level, my soul demanded it. I have learned what is presented in this book through deploying all over the world as a member of the military, through founding businesses that have succeeded and failed, through competing in some of the most brutal athletic events in the world, and through fighting through basic human experiences. And my story is just beginning.

Burn Your Couch is a manifesto for those who wake up every day and know that they are capable of more but can't figure out how to move in the direction that will give them more. Because the basic tenets of success don't change, *Burn Your Couch* is for business owners and employees, athletes and weekend warriors, and anyone interested in finding out who they might be beyond who they are currently. Regardless of what happiness looks like to you, this book contains concrete methods to help you attain it. Or, at a minimum, understand how important it is that you begin stepping toward it.

I have come to realize that nothing in life will force radical growth like taking on a project or an idea that seems beyond your capability at first glance. I have reduced the process to steps and ideas that might help you expand your mind and rethink your approach to such endeavors. I personally prefer the kind of adventures that force growth in order to succeed, which sometimes simply means making it out alive.

I must admit that not all of my ventures have worked out or could be considered successful in a conventional sense. Looking at it all now however, my failures, you will see, were also times of immense growth and learning opportunity. A few decades of trying new things, exploring new ideas, and coming up short has repeatedly taught me that I won't succeed if I don't learn from the experience and live to fight another day. If I internalize both of those things after each new experience, I am primed to transcend by doubling down and coming away with a better result on my next effort. And so are you. So, let's begin, shall we?

Chapter 1. Introduction

"If you end up with a boring miserable life because you listened to your mom, your dad, your teacher, your priest, or some guy on television telling you how to do your shit, then you deserve it."
–Frank Zappa

Have you ever stopped to consider what life is like when it is lived completely inside a virtual world? Your heart will still race occasionally. Whenever the brain sees something it perceives as exciting, it will signal your adrenal medulla to release a shot of the stress-response hormones norepinephrine and epinephrine into your bloodstream. Your pupils will dilate, and for a minute, you will feel really alive. Don't worry; you aren't. Truly feeling alive is always reserved for those in the arena, doing the work. You are just experiencing a physiological response that your ancestors worked into your DNA in order to survive.

In the physical sense, you are alive, but is your soul? That might be another matter altogether. Soon enough, your faculties will realize you are in no real or present danger, and all systems will return to normal. Your heart rate will remain slightly elevated because it isn't used to working hard, but it will be far lower than if you were actually experiencing the things you are consuming on the television. With any luck, you'll be out of the woods of intense experience before you even break a sweat.

Inside your bubble, you have locked down a hell of a spot to finish out your life. You will never have to know defeat. You will never know what it feels like to have a soul-crushing loss, and you will be forever shielded from the cruel emotions that come with failure. You aren't ever going to have to go through the embarrassment of your dreams not working out, and you'll never feel stupid when you go out on a limb and realize you are standing alone because no one followed you.

Food and all necessities to sustain you are within the click of a button. You won't ever be subjected to the harsh realities that lurk outside your door or linger in places outside of the many screens that keep your attention. You can keep tabs on all your friends and family with the various social media platforms, and as long as you don't go too far, you can safely play the role of the critic; that is, you can judge from afar without getting too close to the actual experience. Distance and abstinence are the only ways you can truly guarantee your own safety.

This is life for many people. The comforts listed above have slowly crept into and begun to rule modern Western life. We develop our businesses and choose our activities based on the comfort and ease they can provide. Entrepreneurship has flourished as technology makes life easier every day. The fact is, though, that as we solve problems of discomfort, we are creating new ones. Discomfort has now been put on a slow IV drip. Rather than battle it out with a Saber-toothed tiger, uncomfortable experiences slowly creep into every facet of our lives. They creep so slowly in fact, few of us even know discomfort is present until it has already become habit. Rather, we just know that something within us feels out of sorts. As modern people we are plagued by a host of ailments and neurosis that we struggle to identify and this is because the roots of those problems vanish in the life we've convinced ourselves that we are choosing.

Human evolution depended on the human body's ability to survive and move, and now the human spirit requires those things to feel complete. Many people are now finding out who they become when they ignore that need. Unfortunately, rather than evolution, such a life looks an awful lot like regression. Rather than our lives moving ever upward and filled with inspiration, we become marred by constant deflation.

The way we gobble up every new technological release and service designed to make life easier begs this question: is a life of ease actually the goal? Does easier mean better? An app exists for everything except living a complete life. There is no shortcut to fulfillment. A truly great life requires participation. It requires you to leave the comfort of the bubble that so many of us find ourselves in.

The future is exciting. Artificial intelligence and exponential technologies are revolutionizing our lives in ways we still can't even fathom. We are growing more and more reliant on an ever-evolving set of advances that are undoubtedly changing our lives. New tools are increasing our productivity. New medicines are making health care more affordable for the masses every day. People residing in the developed world are at the epicenter of all of this advancement.

The one thing technology hasn't been able to affect in any lasting way is personal happiness. Research consistently shows that people in the developed Western world are not measurably happier than those who reside in indigenous populations in West Africa. No technology or scientific advance accounts for the human spirit.

Shortcuts to happiness, like drugs and experimental technology, exist, but those are short-lived. The underlying problem interfering with attaining happiness won't be eliminated through drug use or other artificial mood manipulation. Lasting happiness still must be earned.

Humans are flesh and skin held up by a frame of marrow. We are at the mercy of our brains as a command center, albeit an extraordinary one. We still operate with a muscular system at the mercy of an endless set of nerves and synapses, all firing at precisely the correct time to execute complex motor patterns as we lumber through time and space. In essence, the human body is a set of pulleys and levers developed over millions of years of evolution. Our brains, the most complex algorithms imaginable, which update and respond to real time feedback, have been shaped over the same period from billions of "yes, no, and oh sh*t, I took the wrong turn" decisions. Each human feature is a tool born out of a need as we clashed with nature, kicking and clawing our way to the top of the food chain. To think that technology could override something so incredible and complex is naive at best.

The fortune of being composed of matter during this particular speck in eternity while simultaneously being conscious of it is astounding. The literal odds that you have beaten just to arrive here on earth in this now is almost unfathomable. Nothing in the physical world represents those odds in a perceivable, comprehensible way. Zeroes and ones lose their profundity after we lose the ability to comprehend their relative size.

Knowing this, why would anyone celebrate overcoming the most improbable equation by binge-watching Netflix all weekend? I have my theories, and you are going to get most of them throughout this book. At the end of the day, though, lack of thought about the more complex ideas concerning existence squanders the awesome feeling of existence. When you put esoteric notions like this up against bills, late payments, fights with friends, shopping for the latest gadget, and the monotony that competes for our immediate attention, existentialism tends to get pushed aside or swept under the rug. It shows up later as general anxiety.

And in that passage lies the heart of one of our central problems. We are intensely focused on the immediate. We live for gratification in the present time and forgo any real thought about the future. We make decisions based on what will satisfy us now and not on our lasting happiness. We choose the candy bar over waiting for a meal and wonder why we're all so overweight. We choose the orgasm over the committed relationship and then wonder why we feel so lonely. Chasing immediate pleasure can wreak havoc on our long-term well-being.

If, by chance, you do decide to venture outside to look for a better life and equip yourself with the right information, be warned: the world can be daunting when you shed the bubble wrap. For this reason, don't feel like you must have it all figured out. You are going to learn as you go, and in fact, the process of learning is part of a better life. Just start trying to figure out who you really wanted to be and what you really wanted to do before the responsibility and weight of life began to beat the hope out of you.

You don't have to have everything figured out to move forward. At first, you don't need to know where you're going with certainty. You just need to move forward to figure out what else is in front of you. You would be amazed at what you can figure out through exploration. The goal shouldn't be success but action. Run a marathon, write a book, start a business, get fit— just get up and start moving. Stop concerning yourself with what might go wrong or what others might think if you fail. In short, quit leading a life of quiet desperation.

The truth that many people don't want to face is that time is finite. There is no way around this fact. Your clock will expire, and no more time will remain to do all the things that you have always wanted to do. Buying into what you have always been told you should do and putting off what you want to do will not extend that timeline. The question to ask is, when you look back at your life, what are you going to see? I have come to realize that people like to avoid this question, especially people who know that they won't like the answer.

Like it or not, the fact that time is finite means there are many ways to waste something precious. Life does not contain neutral ground. You are always moving toward something; if you aren't deciding what that thing is, then, by default, that thing is choosing you. Every day that goes by, your actions shape your path and direction. In the gym, you can decide to move toward a stronger and more capable frame. On the couch, time and gravity are tugging at your muscles and skin, beckoning you back toward the ground from which you came.

Our hard-fought battle to the top of the food chain has left us with a unique advantage over the rest of the animal kingdom. We are the only animals that get to choose our own evolution. The decisions you make will effectively decide where you go from here. Ernest Becker, in his book *The Denial of Death*, said, "Man is literally split in two: he has an awareness of his own splendid uniqueness in that he sticks out of nature with a towering majesty, and yet he goes back into the ground a few feet in order to blindly and dumbly rot and disappear forever."

An existential bummer, as described by Jason Silva, is the realization that life, everything around us in the physical world, will, in fact, atrophy and die, dissolving into meaningless nothingness. Impermanence applies to everything in this world, and we can do nothing about it. When we start to realize this, how will we react when faced with our own impermanence? How will you react? Should you pretend not to care and search for indifference in life?

Not me, friend. People will come along who claim to know the meaning of life. The only thing I can say with certainty is that no one is certain about the end and, in the end, the only way to find fulfillment in this life is to work toward a mission that aligns with your values. We do not have to agree on the meaning of life to help each other find meaning in life. That last part is why I wanted to write this book.

Don't wait for an existential crisis to start figuring that out. The only thing worse than realizing that life might not matter is realizing you have wasted what little time you were given on things that didn't matter to you.

In the end, if you are blessed with time to reflect, you can look back and see the things you created, the impact you had on the world, the goals you achieved, and your legacy that will live on. Or you can see reruns of your favorite television show. Either option is ultimately your call, but decades from now, your grandkids will be thoroughly unimpressed when you tell them stories about your couch.

Building a life you love is like getting fit

Often, we are guilty of making the unfortunate mistake of thinking we have to get in shape before we can do something we want to do, like play a sport, join a gym, or run a race. I saw this a lot in the world of CrossFit. People wanted to get in shape before they began. The first problem is that "getting in shape" is, at best, loosely defined parameters for a goal, so even tackling that first step isn't achievable in any certain terms. The result is that we get stuck in a self-imposed negative feedback loop, never actually doing what we want to do. The second problem, of course, is that the gym is to get in shape, not just house people who are. Once we understand this, we can explore a new endeavor and accomplish the preparatory step at the same time.

How many things in life do we do this with while the clock ticks away? How often do we force ourselves to the sideline while we wait to fulfill loosely defined goals? The gym in this case was the example, but how many things do you put off until you're ready?

The truth is, you're never going to be ready, and time is going to pass anyway. Even believing you could be ready for the greatness that is your life is an insult to that greatness. Of course you aren't ready. Of course you can still begin.

Burn Your Couch is an antithesis to current popular sentiment. In a society where self-deprecating humor has become prolific on social media, doing nothing has become acceptable or almost noteworthy. Either through marketing genius or unbelievable happenstance, binge-watching television shows has become a badge of honor.

More absurd, we have made a habit of glorifying politicians who run on a platform of a rigged system. Shouting the loudest about being robbed of something has become immensely popular on both sides of the political aisle. It's as if we are all victims and whoever can point their finger first wins. Trying to be the biggest victim is like a race to the bottom of the barrel. Even if you "win," you have accomplished nothing. You were just the quickest to point it out.

The time has come for a revolution and an awakening—at the very least, a shove back at the status quo. The time has come to realize that the things that were originally intended for temporary comfort are bleeding over into aspects of life they don't belong and, as a result, you are missing out on the best version of yourself.

Burn Your Couch is not about living vicariously through anyone else: athletes, actors, or celebrities. You have all the capabilities to do all the things you desire, or you will once you begin the process of a forthright and engaged life. I encourage you to conjure the conviction that you can do all of this because you are alive and have chosen to do so. Don't just think of your couch as the cushion where you crack a beer as your days bleed together in endless monotony. Your "couch" in this sense is the binge-watching of Netflix, settling for a job you don't love because it is the right thing to do, and all the other comforts we tolerate in an attempt to fit in and get along.

Usually, the work toward what you want is not glamorous. It's not always the typical marathon scenario, where people on the side of the road are cheering you on and relishing in your success. Often the reality is the complete opposite of that. The road feels desolate and long, while the obstacles seem overwhelming.

But what is the alternative? Giving up and settling for a life of mediocrity so, somewhere down the line, you can have a life-changing epiphany and realize that the life you have been sold lands you with a life that bores you to death? Or hope that if you trade the minivan in for a convertible and the townhouse for a downtown loft, it will somehow give your life a semblance of what, deep down, you truly want it to be? It won't.

The truth is, people everywhere love the idea of success. They even seem to love the idea of working for it, but the actual act is what tends to weed people out. People love posting a meme on social media that says, "We were not meant to pay bills and die." And then, in an ironic twist of events, they will literally go do just that.

An open letter to those who feel stuck

Of late, there has been a massive shift toward outward reliance. The idea that if things don't work out how you want them to, it must be someone else's fault is massively trending right now. I have seen many people, including friends and family, give up on the life they want because of some deep-seated limitation that they created for themselves. Maybe that limitation is because they don't feel worthy, or maybe it is because they don't feel capable. Regardless, I am positive that it doesn't have to be that way. I have seen so-called ordinary people do incredible things simply because they did not buy into the limiting beliefs that said they couldn't. Rags-to-riches stories are not uncommon, yet people still find themselves trapped in their own self-imposed limitations.

The truth is that your position in life can almost always be improved. It is quite literally never too late to live the life you have always wanted to live or be the person you have always wanted to be. I don't say this as a point of motivation, because upward mobility is a concrete fact of all developed and even slightly capitalistic societies in the twenty-first century, regardless of where you begin from.

The fact that life, by its nature, is extremely unforgiving makes the entire previous paragraph unpopular. When you make terrible choices, you get stuck with terrible results. Sometimes, when you make good choices, you still get stuck with terrible results. Life often feels indifferent to our feelings and emotions about a certain topic. Many people have a really hard time coming to terms with that fact. As a result, they become convinced that life isn't fair and the "system" is rigged against them. In a desperate attempt to make it easier, they give up trying to really get traction toward a life they want, and they begin to settle. They start to blame everything around them for the fact that life isn't working out like they want it to. Soon many different negative feedback loops begin to circulate, and people get into a "rut." These people do not realize that their own toxic thought process and belief system has created the rut in the first place and will, no doubt, keep them there.

It is a deeply human characteristic to look for someone else to solve our problems, so in a sense, we aren't just fighting pop culture, but actual human nature. Fight it with everything you have. Fight it physically by exploring the potential of your body and fight it mentally by surrounding yourself with minds and ideas that energize you.

We have come to a fork in the road. We can choose to fall back into what is comfortable and what has worked in the past, or we can look for new frontiers. Even if your endeavors don't always end up in success, their pursuit ensures that you personally don't end up in a rut. The very nature of exploration requires forward progress, which is the one thing that has the power to keep you from getting stuck.

Escape the hate

It's important to note that if you are ready to start taking a little risk to escape the ordinary, people will hate what you are doing. This next passage is directly related to your relationship with them. If what you are trying to achieve is so grand that small-minded people have trouble accepting its possibility, they will inevitably send misguided frustration your way. Sometimes that will look like hate.

This has absolutely nothing to do with them actually hating you. They hate the life they have settled for or the dreams they have allowed to die and you have become a sounding board for their projections. What's more unfortunate is there is nothing you can do to change their choices or feelings toward you. Some people are wired this way. You can change only your reaction to the nonbelievers. My approach would be to not react at all.

The quickest way to handle small-minded, bitter people is to stop acknowledging them. People don't get a seat at the table in your house simply because they have something to say. Dismiss them. The place you are headed is so far beyond their realm of comprehension, so stopping to acknowledge their plights will do nothing but slow you down. A reason will always exist for why what you are doing will not succeed, and believe me, every jerk out there will point that reason out to you.

The hard truth is that the overwhelming majority of people choose to focus on those reasons and, as a result, sentence themselves to a life of mediocrity. If you are looking for an emotion to feel, feel pity. Most of them will never feel the elation innate with odds-defying achievement.

Every obstacle in the world can be circumnavigated with the right approach, and the further each task takes you out of your comfort zone, the more capable you become as a person. Even if you are not successful at an endeavor in the conventional sense, every attempt, if taken earnestly, provides the opportunity to come back again both stronger and smarter, which is a concept that nonbelievers have not grown enough to gain the capacity to understand.

Adversity will always be a proving ground for the strong

Rarely do I sleep well. Some nights, I will lie in bed for hours, waiting for the alarm clock to go off. Replacing an entire night of sleep with frustration and anticipation makes for a difficult next day. For that reason, I don't hold back when trying to medically induce a coma with sleeping pills. A particularly hot Friday night in Africa in 2010 wasn't any different. I had been on an otherwise eventless deployment for about six months, and I was slowly ticking days off the calendar, biding my time until I could return home to the States.

At nine o'clock that night, I had just taken three sleeping pills and was lying in bed in my hut, waiting for the chemicals to slowly lure me into time travel. Just before they did, I heard an abrupt pounding outside of my door. Whack, whack, whack, each thud grew louder and harder. Then I heard a voice from the other side of the door, "Rick, you awake? Get up. We need your help." As I staggered out my door, feeling half-drunk, I began to try to realize that a frantic girl was saying something about a plane crash and a fire. Feeling a bit like I was standing on sea legs, I slowly put it together. I thought she sounded nuts, and she, no doubt, thought that she was forming cohesive sentences.

From what I gathered, a plane had crashed at the airfield about a mile down the road, and they needed medical support. As I ran over to my gear locker to grab my medical bag, the thought of changing out of my pajamas never crossed my mind. I suppose shorts and a cut-off hoodie seemed as fitting a uniform as any to run directly into chaos. As I snatched my medical bag out of my locker, from the corner of my eye, I caught a red fire extinguisher fastened to the wall. I remembered the girl outside my hut rambling on about a fire, so I grabbed that, too, ran outside, and jumped into the truck that had pulled around for me.

Familiar faces met me, acquaintances I had seen around base in the past few months of deployment to East Africa. We tried to put the story together and figure out where we were going. Apparently, we were driving to the airstrip that was part of the base we were staying at, where a Kenyan Airforce plane had crashed. We put that together just in time to realize it wasn't true. When we pulled up to the tarmac, another Kenyan soldier waved us on to drive to where the crash site supposedly was. This went on for about fifteen miles until we finally ran out of dirt road. Ahead of us, parked in a field next to the woods, were abandoned trucks that must have been full of other people who were now searching for the crash. Apparently, they had left the vehicles and begun hiking through the jungle. A little bit late to the party, we did the same.

We hiked for what felt like hours. Sort of…

The African jungle is a bit less than welcoming when it comes to a hike. The ground was slippery and muddy. Large rocks blocked the trail, and the trees grew horizontal to the ground after only a few feet of upward growth. Before long, the thick jungle forced our hike into a crawl.

As the thorns tore at my bare legs, we had two ways of knowing where we were going. One was to radio air support, which was attempting to vector us to the site by flying toward the crash. We crawled in one direction for thirty minutes, heard a loud noise overhead, turned sharply in the direction the plane flew, and kept crawling. Our second means was to follow the voice of the Kenyan soldier leading the quickly deteriorating mission. He would yell into the night, and the hope was that eventually the crash victims would hear him and the night would yell back. Neither of these plans was effective or efficient, but in the moment, you use what you have. We paid dearly for the flawed logic of our thrown-together plan.

As the hours began to drag on, the voices of the people who had come out with me began to reflect the desolation of the jungle. First came the audible prayers. One of the corpsmen started to take notice of the fact that we were going deeper and deeper into the African jungle, which is where the biggest cats in the world live. "Rick, I know you're not religious, man, but I'ma pray for you, too," he said. "We out here, and there's a bunch of things that want to kill us." The sight of a lion crossing the road as we were leaving the compound a day earlier certainly didn't help matters. Neither did the stories of a drunk Kenyan soldier who had passed out on his lawn, only to be dragged off into the woods and never seen alive again.

Another corpsman, who was assigned to a different unit on base and had woken me up, had also come out to play that night. She was no longer having any fun, either. Her whimpers became louder, and her pleas for reassurance grew more desperate until she progressed to what felt like a full-on breakdown, crying, "We aren't ever going to get out of the woods."

Now, I'll be the first to admit we were in the midst of a suck-fest. My legs were torn apart from thorns and rocks, my forearms were spent from dragging an oversized industrial fire extinguisher with me, and I was growing ever more frustrated with every branch that caught my clothes or snagged my medical bag, leaving me to collect my trauma equipment in the dark. I was sick of crawling, and not lost on any of us was the fact that if we ever did find the crash site, survivors were surely no longer survivors. I will honestly say, though, in the middle of listening to the people around me showing no signs of coping with adversity, I was experiencing some different emotions.

The first thought I had was to notice my focus. I felt a bit impressed by my ability to stay locked in mentally on what mattered and let go of what could not be controlled. The second thought I had was, *Holy sh*t, I'm prepared for this.* I was not necessarily prepared for the mission—wearing pajamas, lugging a useless fire extinguisher, and carrying a half-empty medical bag—but I couldn't have been more mentally and physically ready. Seven years earlier, while going through a Naval Special Warfare selection course, I had thought the whole thing was stupid. The instructors yelling needlessly, the long days and sore muscles, the soft-sand runs and underwater evolutions that felt like they were never going to end—I had hated so much of it, but now, in this moment of chaos, I couldn't have been more appreciative.

When I think back on that night and many like it, I go back to what our class mentor told us during selection, after a particularly tough evolution: "Look around. Notice how many empty chairs we have in this classroom." He gestured at the chairs that used to seat the people who had just quit. "There will be something here that is really hard for you during training. We don't just run, we don't just swim, we don't just run obstacle courses, we don't just do physical training, and we don't just have classes. We do all of these things because we want to test you and, chances are, one of those things is going to reveal a weakness. I don't give a shit if you are a good runner in soft sand. I just want to know whether you are the guy who is going to quit when his back is against the wall. We want guys who can do anything, run through a f*cking brick wall if that's what it takes. So far, everyone still sitting in here has what it takes."

I required being tested in the real world to figure out who I was. Everyone around me fell apart, and I knew that I was the one who kept it together. The lessons we forge in our life are all we will have to fall back on when times get tough, and unfortunately, we have no idea when that might be. If a tougher situation were to arise, I do not know if I would handle it with similar poise. What I do know is that I could not go back and get more training at that moment. I could not go back and get in better shape or become tougher or more resilient. All I had was what I had gathered up until that point. That's all any of us ever have.

The thoughts and concepts in this book might be counterintuitive to what you read elsewhere. These concepts aren't theory or useless drivel meant to entertain. I fought for these lessons. I have suffered for these lessons, and I want you to suffer too. Not because I don't like you but because there is great value found in suffering. Despite pop culture and intrusive marketing, you can thrive in today's world. You can grow healthy in a world that has normalized sickness. Strong, in a world that has accepted weakness.

Chapter 2. Purpose

*"Purpose is only revealed to those with the courage to
step toward an intrinsically meaningful life."
– Me, after realizing that true purpose would never be
found outside of myself.*

Animals need purpose. Huskies need a sled to
pull, or they can become lazy. Lions need prey to chase,
or they starve, and humans need a mission to focus their
energy, or they become irritable, waste time, and focus
on trivial things that do not matter—only they don't
know these trivial things don't matter, because they
haven't a clue about what does matter. Purpose is a fact
of life that cannot be ignored. When you step back and
take a look at the world, you realize that the need for
purpose is the single driving force behind everything in
life. The degree to which it drives something, however,

is completely dependent upon the relative relationship between the entity driving and its destination.

The understanding of this single fact will allow you to look at the world through a completely different lens and is the key to freedom from the distractions that seek to own your bandwidth. When you know what is for you, it is much easier to ignore what is not. Purpose gives you the unique ability to look at the world for what it has the possibility to be and not for what it currently is. Those who shape the world in this manner can begin to change it. Doing that requires changing yourself, which is impossible without knowing what currently guides you. In other words, we are transformed in pursuit of our purpose.

Purpose is the reason something is done or created or for which something exists. Although not the most complex concept to understand, the pursuit of purpose has created existential crises in the human heart for generations. A deeper understanding of purpose puts an individual far ahead of others who do not have that understanding. Furthermore, the more aligned with your purpose you become, the less likely it is that outside factors can influence your outcome or derail you from the outcome you truly want. Alignment with purpose allows you to make decisions that move you toward what you want. Delaying gratification is easier if you know why. Saying yes or no to opportunities becomes easier when the answer is based on purpose rather than emotion.

Through an intense and, at times, misplaced desire to leave my mark on the world in business, I discovered I was unknowingly putting a massive restriction on myself. As much as a younger version of myself would hate to admit it, achievement for the sake of possessions turns out to be a crummy motivator for a customer base when the grind really sets in. And if what you are trying to do is worth a damn, the grind will set in. Furthermore, the ability to show fortitude when times are tough is also a distinguishing factor between people who succeed in tough endeavors and people who do not. Recognizing this will hopefully inspire you to seek a deeper purpose than the three superficial reasons most people have for undertaking a project: money, sex, and power. You may want these things. You may also want to know what they mean and what part of you feels incomplete if you don't have them. Somewhere in there, you might find a purpose that lasts.

The best part about having a purpose that really resonates with you is that it gives you the power to confidently say no, which is a primary influence on success. When I first started my supplement company, though I wouldn't admit it, what I actually wanted was to hang out with models and fly on a private jet. What I didn't understand at the time was that sex and money are awful foundational values to build a great organization on. Because I didn't have a central purpose grounded in anything of real value, I was poised to make mistake after mistake. I tried to emulate what big players in the space did. I sponsored athletes and paid to get myself on the headline of bigger competitions. I became a watered-down replica of bigger companies that I perceived as better companies.

What I began to find is that a business or organization is not unlike a person in that, the more aligned it is with its purpose, the more effective and efficient its daily activities are. A powerful mission statement that resonates with employees and customers has the strength to pull a business through many difficult situations and help it make decisions that are aligned with its central purpose. As I began to look for new growth opportunities and improve stalling sales, I came to the realization that if I truly wanted to be successful, I was going to have to do the uncomfortable thing and figure out what I really wanted, not to mention what I wanted the function of my business to be outside of making money.

Realizing that your business is driving along without a road map can be unsettling when you are pouring your heart and soul into it. This single realization inspired me to not only seek out the driving force behind my actions, but to also research the driving force behind the actions of everything around me. What I found was that people and organizations with purposes that were bigger than themselves were the recipients of aiding forces that were also bigger than themselves.

Had I had a refined vision like I do now (having no money will force you to quickly figure out what matters), I would have easily seen that those things truly weren't important or even realistic. The big players could hire athletes and influencers with a big-enough following to get a return on their investment, and they had the money to experiment when that didn't work out. My goal was to aid people's active pursuits by providing products without fillers and prioritizing people's well-being needs through content production and education. Creating great content costs nothing but time. It sure would have been nice to say no to those things I didn't actually need. At least, my bank account would have appreciated it.

The 2008 movie *Yes Man* depicts a motivational speaker who casts a spell on Carl, a character played by Jim Carrey, effectively making him incapable of saying no. The movie shows a life that is transformed from miserable to fulfilling, effectively giving Carl the love of his life and a ton of new friends simply because he says yes to every opportunity that presented itself. As the movie winds on, however, just like all great rom-coms, the plot begins to twist. Some of the things that he had said "yes" to on a whim begin to catch up to him, and he comes to a lonely halting point.

Carl presents us with a great life lesson. At first, you should say yes to the opportunities around you. By doing so, you'll get to know both yourself and the world better. You should get off your couch and explore and do things. Do everything that sounds fun or interesting or that you feel drawn to, even though you can't articulate why (the soul will often nudge us before we know why).

As each new experience allows you to grow, however, you have to refine the number of things you say yes to. Do less of what you don't like and more of what feels like it aligns with you. Every experience you move through will help you grow closer to the person you want to be as you find the experiences that resonate with who you truly are. That, my friend, is where you will find your purpose.

The evolution of purpose

"We are proud primates drawn to shiny, gigabit-rich gizmos, no money-down guarantees, the promise of rapid ascension, and rightfully so, the amazing abundance of knowledge in the age of Wikipedia."

Burn Your Couch

–Chris Moore, Way Past Strong

If you had been born in the Stone Age, about two and a half million years ago, you would certainly not have been concerned with notions such as "finding yourself" or "figuring out what you are here for." You would have worked diligently to chip tools out of rock that would, hopefully, allow you to get a leg up on the rest of the ecosystem and the food chain. You would have moved in a fashion that was much more directed by your sympathetic nervous system, which is also known as the fight-or-flight mechanism. Your purpose stared you straight in the face in the form of Darwinian theory every single day.

Taking the path of least resistance has been vital to our survival as a species from the very beginning. When you are fighting for everything you have, including food and shelter, wasting energy and looking for extra work just doesn't make sense. Quite literally, using the minimum amount of effort when you could helped ensure your continued existence.

The unfortunate irony is that life no longer innately demands that same level of effort. To feel that level of success in the modern age, you have to be willing to go out and find it. You must fight the instinct not to look for extra work. If you do not, you will get the intended result of your default wiring, which is that you will simply exist. In the Stone Age, existence had meaning because simply existing was the meaning. Today, not so much.

Now we in the developed Western world have made existing so easy that doing only that no longer provides purpose or fulfillment. I'm not saying this is all bad; in fact, quite the opposite. Since we have the whole existence thing under control, barring some kind of self-imposed catastrophe, we are free to pursue higher things. We can figure out what we really identify with and pursue it with all of our being. We owe it to ourselves to embrace this new era in our evolution. We can choose to fall back into what is comfortable and what has worked, or we can go out looking for new frontiers. The opportunity to make an impact on the world in a way that aligns with your values has never been greater.

We are now freer to search for purpose than we've ever been in history. The evolution of our prefrontal cortex and the ability to process complex thought has freed humans to solve nonlinear problems and look for purpose in new places. People are trying to cure terrible diseases and provide educational opportunities where they've previously never existed, yet as a society, we have the audacity to present the world with a skyrocketing depression rate that borders on an epidemic. We have an incredible opportunity, and we, myself included, should make a conscious decision to start acting like it.

The modern purpose

Traditional schooling in Western culture can be incredibly efficient when it comes to creating terribly obedient machines. When you look at it through the lens of purpose, this efficiency makes sense. In the late-seventeenth century, formal schooling was introduced to the United States for the betterment of society and the forward progress of the collective. And you know what society needs? It needs cogs. Cogs keep the machine moving. Personally, I have always rejected the notion of becoming a cog. The very thought of being average has always bothered me more than I care to admit (hence the title of this book). It's not that I feel I am better than other people; it's just that I feel better than me. I know I am capable of more, if that makes sense. Thinking in new ways and finding purpose beyond what you're given can be great ways to figure out what "more" means to you.

Change can be rapid if you are open to it

I was somewhere in Africa, and it was hot, like, really hot. My body kept me nice and oiled up with a sheen of sweat as my shirt stuck to me in all the wrong areas. Just when I thought I might be getting comfortable, a slow bead of sweat would roll down my back and into my waistline, letting me know I was still in Africa.

Burn Your Couch

I was sitting in a small airport in the middle of a rolling, dusty plain, on a six-hour layover for a flight to what would be my fourth deployment in the military. I harbored a very rational fear of consuming the food and water, the result of my last trip to Africa when I'd lost seventeen pounds very quickly from a rare bacterial infection that had held its ground against the strongest antibiotics.

I went to search the small airport for something to occupy me, and this was when Africa changed my entire life, as the continent does in various ways for many visitors. Reaching into an old bin full of dusty books, I picked up *Rich Dad Poor Dad*, by Robert Kiyosaki. This book packed more punch in a few hundred pages than my previous sixteen years of formal education. I realized that the limits on what I could do and build in this lifetime were largely fictional. More than that, the book opened the floodgates and made me starve for more personal growth. I read all the classics, *Think and Grow Rich*, *The 7 Habits of Highly Effective People*, *How to Win Friends and Influence People*, and the list went on.

Burn Your Couch

All these books, though different in nature, pointed to a very similar theme: the rules we are told we must adhere to are really only half of the story. The other half is how you think about them. We don't have to live and die as part of someone else's plan. This concept changed my entire view of purpose and made me acutely aware of the fact that rather than be a cog in a machine, I wanted to spend my time learning how to operate the machine, if not build it.

Earl Nightingale, one of the earliest speakers on the topic of success, defined it as the gradual realization of a worthy ideal. When looked at in this light, success is not the summit of a high mountain but the continual ascent and descent of the many mountains you feel compelled to climb. Eventually, with every mountain you conquer or fall short of conquering, you begin to get a better picture of the ones really worth climbing, and this is where greater and greater success is found. You find that your life is a series of peaks and valleys, but the beauty is you get to choose which ones.

Chapter 3. Happy > Normal

"Times of transition are strenuous, but I love them. They are an opportunity to purge, rethink priorities, and be intentional about new habits. We can make our new normal any way we want."
–Kristin Armstrong

Humans do a lot of crazy things to not look crazy to other humans. Masking our true selves is a stigma that develops for most of us at some point around puberty. The worst thing in the world when you're growing up is to be regarded as an outcast. As the genetic lottery sorts itself out, people begin to fall into their roles. Some of us bully others, labeling someone else before anyone has time to label us. Some of us get bullied and just hope for once to get through the day without getting looked at as different. Extroverts tend to draw people's attention, making them more popular than their peers. Introverts rarely speak up and keep their genius hidden from the normalcy of everyday life. Some fly the freak flag early, attempting to get ahead of opinions in a bold way. Others learn to dismantle themselves and beat everyone else to the punch so they fit in in a self-deprecating way.

Although this is magnified during the years of development, not much changes as adults. The stakes get higher, of course. Doing "normal" things, like going to college, begin to require acquiring debt. Getting a "normal" nine-to-five job may tug at your soul a bit, but what are a few compromises in the name of normalcy, right? And so, the game perpetuates.

We self-impose others' expectations on us and then spend much of the precious time we have here on earth trying to live up to those expectations. We often feel guilty and shame ourselves when we don't live up to these expectations, which were actually never ours to carry. The net result is that we use a disproportionate amount of our resources on things we don't actually value.

Surely, there are things you want to do or accomplish before you reach the pearly gates? Many of us don't pursue those things because the dreams in our soul may ask us to do things that are considered pretty far from normal to attain what will satisfy. And since we have spent virtually all of our life ignoring these types of things, the path we want is unacceptable by our own standard. We may have to live on little means to bootstrap a business. We may have to drop out of college for a business that requires everything from us. We may have to risk whatever we have for a dream no one else can see or, as a result, condone.

The value of your thoughts

We come from a lineage of assimilating into a tribe. In our primitive years as a species, hunting and working in tribes made a lot of sense. Surviving a world full of both animals and deadly elements is just easier when you can split up the work. Even now, studies have shown that people who have a sense of community are happier, healthier, and tend to live longer.

Companies such as Apple and CrossFit have been successful in large part because they have created a tribe to which people love to belong. But just like many of the things we were accustomed to doing as we evolved, tribalism isn't the end of our story. We always have to search for ways to walk the thin line between tradition and growth. We can never let the evolution that got us where we are now hold us back from getting to where we truly want to be. At the same time, we must acknowledge what we've gone through so we don't repeat it.

We should never settle for what other people think, when we have not yet explored the thoughts on our own. This is where we find our original genius and where so much creativity and growth tend to be found. The problem is that we are so exposed to bias throughout life that overcoming it is near impossible. Most of us have thoughts that are recycled from the people around us, whose thoughts are just recycled from the people around them. And the whole world continues this way, with no one making any meaningful kind of change or equitable contribution. Then, one day, a Steve Jobs type comes along with an original idea, and just like that, we are awakened to a different thought pattern. We find a new tribe.

The only way I have found to break free of this paradigm is to expose my mind to many different ways of thinking and many different experiences. Many people use psychedelics and plant medicines to force the shift in perspective, to tear the mainframe out, so to speak. Many of us attend seminars or read books that nudge us along. Still, many of us never get to the point of originality at all. We just grow up and grow old, never knowing how we truly feel or what we truly think about anything.

Many people feel strongly about topics about which they know nothing. They are just repeating headlines and social media memes and getting worked up when someone challenges what their tribe believes. You see it with nationalism, you see it with politics, and you see it with religion. We vehemently protect the thoughts of our tribes, though our lives no longer depend on them.

Furthermore, as a society, we look down upon people who change their minds. In politics, we call them "flip-floppers." In real life, people get frustrated when you don't fit in the little box they have manufactured for you, and they would much rather that you just keep on believing what they believe, as if entrenchment in an opinion about a certain topic, to never learn or grow, is productive.

The people who mine the contents of their own soul for originality are the trendsetters. The ones who spark the initial thought pattern become the central tribal figure, and this is precisely where the idea of value in an original thought lies. People will line up and pay every cent they have if they can be part of a community that resonates with original thinking. The catch is that you have to think differently than your tribe to form one in the first place.

A little defiance is always in order

"He was a man that had accepted the creed that no one had the right to stop him."
–Ayn Rand

Right and wrong can be awfully constricting social constructs. I don't say this to advocate an abolishment of morals, but instead to posit a reframing of definitions. As an example, consider the word "disruptive," which is typically reserved for those in the back of the class who are constantly getting other kids to laugh, acting up, and distracting the teacher with their antics. We are conditioned to have an unfavorable view of disruptive people. When those disruptors grow up to be Steve Jobs and create Apple, a company that has repeatedly disrupted entire industries, we seem to be a little more conservative with our condemnation.

Could it be, instead, that little Stevie, who couldn't stop challenging the teacher and thinking out loud in the back of the class, wasn't so bad after all? Maybe we just had him playing the wrong game in the first place. When Michael Jordan took on baseball, the world didn't say he was a bad athlete.

Defiance is the very seed from which innovation grows. It allows us to see things not as they are, but for what they have the possibility to be. For many of us left-brainers, it can be easy to settle for a life of spreadsheets and perfect order, leaving the real creativity to the naturally gifted. As many of us know, however, life isn't black and white like that. To spawn creativity, you may have to be willing to do the opposite of what you are told, at least in the mind. We must question outcomes, processes, and facts if they do not sit right with us. In any given situation, allow yourself to reframe it. The most successful people in life don't know everything, and they don't need to. They just need to be willing to ask the right questions, or in society's eyes, the wrong ones.

Defiance is the outcome of the ability to look beyond your current situation. It is the ultimate act of freedom because, when you defy something, you are no longer bound by the constraints of your surroundings. Defiance subconsciously scares the hell out of people because the outcome they receive is a direct reflection of the choices they have made. On the contrary, "doing what you're told" is often a convenient scapegoat for adverse results. This way of thinking causes fear when the possibility of failure becomes real, and often we begin looking for places to offload blame. If you have defied your critics and made the decision to go out on your own, no one else is to blame if things don't work out.

Coincidently, this is also a situation that needs a little reframing. If you go against the grain and fail, the answer is never to head back to the herd, hoping that no one saw your misguided bravery. The answer is to reflect on what you've learned, invest in yourself, and double down. Failure is learning. This is not to deny the odds, but rather to say that when you try to defy them, failure is an inevitable part of that process. Just like everything else, success is a process. Take mental or physical stock of what you learned, reshape and redesign your plan, and get back to work. Silicon Valley has a common theme of failing fast and failing often because failure is the only sure path that leads to eventual success when it is traveled long enough.

One of the attributes that draws us to romanticize and look up to professional and elite-level athletes is that they defy our previously conceived notions of what we believed was humanly possible. There was a time in history when it was believed to be physically impossible to run a mile in under four minutes. Roger Bannister had the audacity to defy that notion, clocking a mile in 3:59.4. When this limitation no longer existed, it was not long before many people suddenly possessed this superhuman ability. The kicker, though, is that no one can tell you the name of the second person to run a mile in less than four minutes, because he was no longer defying what we thought of as possible; he was merely replicating what had been done. The history books are overflowing with the names of people who either defied what was thought to be possible or dared valiantly enough to attempt to defy it. What they don't contain are the names of people who got a taste of failure and concluded that success was not for them. Failure may ask you to pivot, it may ask you to retool your approach, and it may ask you to open your mind and heart to new ways of being, but it does not ask you to quit. That is a uniquely human thought.

If you have a vision for your life that is anything outside of what society would consider normal or conventionally acceptable, you need to get real comfortable with the idea of defiance. According to

Forbes Magazine, around ninety percent of all small businesses fail. What this means is that you have to get comfortable with a certain level of defiance just to enter the arena. You are attempting to defy odds that are certainly not in your favor. Everything in life has an associated risk. Our job, then, is not to avoid risk, but rather to get comfortable navigating it, to dance with it.

Fate isn't what you think it is

"Until you make the unconscious conscious, it will direct your life and you will call it fate."
–Carl Jung

The idea of growth brings to the surface the idea of fate. As you grow internally, you become aware that your perceived possibilities are also growing, and you wonder what those old limitations were made of. Bad ideas? Other people's ideas? A false understanding of self? And if you grow into this, could you maybe grow into that? Where exactly do the outer limits lie? You begin to get the idea that we truly have no idea what humans are capable of.

Conversely, when you are growth-minded but having trouble reaching whatever you perceive the next level of growth to be, it can feel like your fate is pressing down upon you, holding you in place. I have spent an uncomfortable amount of time becoming intimately familiar with the person I do not want to be. For many of us, it feels like the harder we push back against the tide, the swifter the water flows in the direction that we do not want to go. I have spent much of my time trying to commit to a new kind of life, only to slide back into my normal routine and old habits, and I can't help but feel like the deck is somehow stacked against me. I say this, however, to highlight the danger in simply believing what you think based on what you feel. The truth is, we are held captive far more by the patterns we've deemed "normal" than we are reality.

People by and large do believe in fate. That's why the expression "everything happens for a reason" is so commonly used. Such expressions can help cultivate faith, which can help you weather the many storms you'll go through in your path of becoming. One thing that faith can gift you with is the internal strength to shoulder external pain and find purpose in that pain. It gives you a way of understanding that pain, regardless of how intense it might be, does not have the final say in your story. Faith is trust in the unfolding of a bigger picture, even when your current picture feels as though it is growing ever so compressed.

At this point, pain actually takes on a redemptive quality, and the forces that seek to bring you in a negative direction begin to lose their charge. Everything then becomes in service to the best version of yourself, which is the best-case scenario for the world you inhabit. Viktor Frankl, Holocaust survivor, said: "Man can take on any suffering as soon and as long as he can find meaning in it."

That being said, when faith is used as a reason to abdicate work or responsibility, it can be just as harmful as it is helpful. Faith, like anything in life, can always be misdirected and used inappropriately. At it's best, faith helps you find meaning and shoulder incredible heartache along the way. At its worst, it is used as a crutch to avoid the pain that occurs when taking personal responsibility. Regardless of your belief in a higher power, having a say in the way you show up in the world is productive and empowering to believe, so for this book, I would like to keep our focus here. The easy road of victimhood is always enticing to our lower selves. Faith in yourself, your abilities, and the life you're building can be difficult.

As a quick note, I have often witnessed that people feel as though, if they have faith in God, it can—and often should—replace faith in self. The result is that you end up waiting on a ship to come in, never realizing you were the captain the whole time. If your belief system does include faith in God, it is helpful to understand that God made you, which means your capabilities have been sewn into the fabric of who you are. Your faith, then, is in some part trust that your creator did not err in forming the person you are. In a self-deprecating world, this can be tough.

Much of the way life turns out—the good and bad fortune and the explainable and seemingly unexplainable—are often results of choices you have made, some independently and some cumulatively. In many cases, we don't pick up on that fact because the results are so far downstream from the choices we've made that we've forgotten how we've crafted the world we're in. It can also be helpful to admit that just because you don't understand the equation, it doesn't mean the solution is outside your control. Neil deGrasse Tyson said it well: "The universe is under no obligation to make sense to you."

Whether you identify with creation or evolution plays no role in determining where you shake out in destiny unless you are looking to outsource your power to a belief system. If you can own your life, from the mistakes and blunders to the triumphs and achievements, you will be the one calling the shots—at least, to the degree that anyone can call the shots in their life. If you rely and place blame on others, you will be easily used as a prop in the planning of someone else's destiny.

How-to articles get a massive click-through rate. Everyone is always seeking the quick solution to a problem. We want the answers laid out in front of us as if the best things in life, the achievements that are reserved for the dedicated and hardworking, can just be served up on a silver platter. They cannot. If you Google how to do most anything, an article will pop up with that same title. This is how marketers take advantage of the weakest parts of the buying public: the parts that are desperately searching for someone else with the answers so we can be spared the work required to solve a problem or complete a task.

The how-to articles are sexy for sure, but real life is more gritty than that. When it comes to explaining fate, the truth isn't flashy, either. The profound lies in simplicity. Every single day, you are faced with small decisions. Over time, those decisions begin to form a pattern that ultimately becomes a habit. Are you in the habit of going to the gym after work or taking the shortest route to your couch so you can unwind? Regardless, that habit comes from a decision that you have made time and time again until you actually aren't making the decision anymore; you're on autopilot. Then it is your old decisions that are making you.

All of these habits were once formed from the slightest decisions you made, and now they have come together to build your routine. This is the matter that forms your life. Our routines built on habits occupy daily life. Whatever you become in this life, these routines end up shaping your destiny. The nightly beer on the couch, the small-minded conversations that are centered in gossip and not ideas, and the days that all melt into each other because there is nothing differentiating the first day of the week from the last aside from a two-day reprieve from your job are some of the things that make up a lackluster fate. If you continue making the simple and easy choice, defaulting to your own default, you may end up going quite far down a boring road.

The irony is that people will live the exact life I just described and then say how difficult achieving what you really want in life is. The truth is, most people don't even know how difficult capturing something extraordinary is because they have never deviated their routine or set it up correctly to align with what they want. In other words, they haven't tried it, so they do not know. Most people unconsciously view even the slightest routine change to be an affront to their comfort. This is one reason many people resist change so ferociously, even though it is change that holds all the answers to the question of who you can become. If you want to have even a bit more say in what your fate looks like, you simply have to consciously make the smallest decisions in your life. These are what will lead your life to a different place.

I have spent hours thinking about the validation I might receive from becoming a *New York Times* bestseller. In fact, I have thought so much about the end of the story that I flew past the middle altogether. One thing you'll notice is that your hopes and goals are often based on what other people have when you are making your decisions unconsciously. This is because you literally have not tuned in enough to yourself to know what *you* actually want. Consciousness now is how we build a better tomorrow.

To state the obvious, a book will not be written simply because I fantasize about how many people will buy it. Instead, I've had to spend hours pouring myself into the keyboard, stressing my mind in every direction, all while knowing that a large portion of what I write will eventually be thrown out as I mine the contents of my soul for something you might be able to relate to and use in your life. In light of this fact, it was the pouring out of the soul that I had to fall in love with. Ironically, once I did, the bestseller list meant less and less.

Whatever title or achievement you may think you want will provide little solace when you are sacrificing day in and day out in service to a higher goal and self. And you must sacrifice because only a thief would expect something for free. Our values and the worthiness of our goals make the demand for what must be given up. Much of what we want to accomplish in life is this way. We must commit to searching tirelessly for the diamonds buried within the mud of the mundane, and we must sacrifice our desire for the simplicity of autopilot.

High performers commit to a lifestyle of small differences, and those differences are a catalyst for a completely different life over time. They approach every rep in life as if it is their first, and they appreciate it like it is their last. Nothing is taken for granted as they practice elevating the mundane. In essence, they learn to ritualize the process.

This desire to elevate the mundane through ritual is buried deep within the human psyche. It accounts for Abraham building an altar to the Lord in some of the very first recorded stories we have. It is also the impulse that lies at the center of the athlete who has special shoelaces for games and does not wash their practice jersey. To ritualize and elevate the mundane is to look at the life you are given and say:

"Even this shall be considered sacred."

"Even this shall be a building block to greater glory."

"Even this, which a million others may have dismissed as inconsequential, matters."

Through the right decisions in service to the right goal, people slowly perfect their craft. They take advantage of lucky breaks as their preparation is met with timing. Eventually, if they are persistent enough, they become an overnight success after two decades of hard work.

In the pursuit of becoming greater, it is easy to feel overwhelmed. The feeling that simply too much exists to accomplish ends many people's ambitions of self-improvement before they begin. Bringing your focus back to the present action is a good way of working through it. For this, I recommend what has been called the *domino effect*. The *domino effect* refers to a sequence of events that starts with a very small change. With everything going on in life, the single most important thing that would have the greatest impact on your goals is your first domino.

Beginning with one small domino, you can knock over another that is fifty percent larger. A two-inch domino can knock over a three-inch domino. A three-inch domino can then knock over a four-and-a-half-inch domino. If you continued with this linear progression, by the thirty-first domino, you would be able to knock over one taller than the Eiffel Tower. The fifty-seventh domino would stretch so tall that you would literally be able to bridge the gap between the earth and the moon. ANYONE can make fifty-seven strategic steps toward the life they want. Remember this when your goals feel as far away as the moon.

Consider the one thing you could accomplish today, right now, that moves the needle the most. If you want to go back to being overwhelmed and worried, that option will always be there. Try focusing on that first step and leveraging physics rather than fighting a fate you don't understand. This strikes me as a much more pragmatic way to go about getting what you want. Forget about conquering the moon for now; focus on the first domino, the one directly in front of you.

Another issue with feeling locked into a certain fate is that it is just that, a feeling. Until you've really learned to sit with your intuition, feelings can be extremely unreliable. All these feelings about what you can accomplish in life are typically nothing more than manufactured limitations based on factors such as how you were raised and what you have experienced. If one of your parents was an Olympic athlete, you are much more prone to believing that competing in the Olympics is something possible for you. If you are like me, you have never known anyone who competed in the Olympics, so it is likely that you believe being an Olympic athlete isn't even a remote possibility. You can apply this example to many things in life: running a business, going to college, completing a marathon, etc...

I certainly dealt with this imposter syndrome as I embarked on a special operations career in the military. I had never known anyone to do such a thing, and as a result, I had very little confidence in my own ability to succeed. The needed confidence, however, was gifted to me as I engaged with the process through my selection phase of training. (This is the phase where attrition is the highest, as most people quit or end up dropped for lack of performance or injury.) Every day that I did not quit, I saw that it became more likely that I might make it to graduation. Halfway through the program, I knew there was nothing in the world that could make me quit. Now, looking back over a decade of service, I see how my first notions were really just misguided limiting beliefs that had very little to do with my actual capabilities. Thank God I stuck it out long enough to find out what they actually were.

I advise you to take a closer look at what you base your life upon. What is the source of your values, thoughts and beliefs? Lacking this examination, you could end up living your entire life based on a set of limitations that don't even exist. Maybe you have not had access and exposure to their alternative. This may be one reason Plato is credited with saying, "An unexamined life is not worth living."

I personally have every intention of finding out where the real limits lie. I want to die knowing what I am capable of accomplishing, what my body is capable of doing, and what my mind is capable of creating. I want to die having maxed out this one opportunity at life. As with the book example above, however, this won't happen because I simply say it, believe it, or want it. I have to start taking all of the little daily steps, some of which are quite uncomfortable. Fight through the limitations that you believe encompass your fate so you can see the life waiting for you on the other side. There is no greater feeling than watching the world open up to you as you learn to engage with it earnestly.

To do this is to level up. To level up means to reach a higher state of performance or being. It is typically done by rising to the caliber of your surroundings. Jim Rohn was the first to say that you are the average of the five people with whom you spend the most time, and since then, motivational speakers everywhere have been using some twist on that expression. This is because the wisdom rings true no matter how much society evolves. Your annual salary, your worldview, your hobbies, and your lifestyle design almost always match the people with whom you associate the most.

You may also find that you have to level up without the squad, or you all have to level up together. Otherwise, you'll find your surroundings consistently seek to pull you back down to maintain homeostasis. This isn't said out of malice and is not an attempt to rid you of your friends. People simply grow and evolve in different directions. That doesn't mean you have to drop friends and loved ones who aren't dedicated to the same growth you are; it means you have to limit exposure to people who have no intention of going where you are going. Otherwise, you are likely to never get there. This is not only true for who you are around but also *what* you are around. Every single thing injected into your consciousness will take up some sort of residency in your being. We often don't understand this when our results are disconnected from our informational diet.

From time to time, I harbor an unhealthy obsession with watching the news, as I hope to be informed and know what is going on in the world. The problem with consuming any type of media is that you are almost always consuming an agenda. In some cases, we overlook the slant specifically because it confirms our own bias and provides a feeling of comfort. For-profit news corporations have made an entire industry out of grabbing viewers' attention with outrage, playing on their fears, and forcing them to wait and see how it all turns out. Every news cycle, the story changes, but the theme does not.

It took me far too long to realize that I have other options. Alternative conversations are taking place that are much more conducive to positive discourse and finding the truth, which is almost always somewhere between the poles. Those conversations are taking place on podcasts, in books, and at conferences all over the world. And speaking of the world, it isn't going to end. Or maybe it is, but in any case, constant worry isn't going to change that. It will, however, derail you from your goals, making it less likely that you'll adequately cultivate your gifts. The quality of your life simply is not worth their bottom line.

If you don't believe me, try this experiment: cut yourself off completely from mainstream media for thirty days. No consumption of current events whatsoever. Social media is difficult, I know. Just unfollow anything that pops up with the news. Don't worry; they will all be there in a month, and by that time, the sky will be falling in a different way should you decide you can't live without them. After a month goes by, pick your poison and turn on CNN, Fox, or NBC and put it on mute with subtitles. For some reason, when you are reading the words, the outrage and fear they hope to inspire become more obvious.

I stumbled upon this experiment when I spent a month training on a remote island off the coast of Mexico. As I sat in LAX on the return trip, I was reading the subtitles that came across CNN. After breaking free from my desensitization to their tactics, I couldn't help but feel that I was living in some alternate reality where human welfare was put so far below the profit motive that it truly wasn't a consideration at all.

Simply put, if you want to create a life that you're going to have to grow into, you can't afford to consistently max out your bandwidth with the worst the world has to offer. You only have so much. And because your window of potential grows smaller with every moment that goes by, the cost associated with your attention rises every day.

The powers that be and alchemy

Every four years, the United States votes on a politician who will become the leader of the free world, and every four years, Americans fight and clamor to lay out a case for why their backed candidate will make a positive change for the country. In eighth-century Europe, Arabian settlers brought the craft of alchemy to Western culture. Focusing on the spiritual and metaphysical world, an alchemist would move from town to town, promising the townspeople that they would be able to turn rocks to gold and even create a potion capable of immortality—for a fee. In return, the townspeople would give the alchemist money and wait patiently for the alchemist to transform their lives. Eventually, when no change occurred and the alchemist could no longer hold off the mobs of people screaming sham, the townspeople would run the alchemist out of town. The alchemist would then repeat the process at the next town.

The net result was that an alchemist became wealthy by exploiting the human desire for a quick fix to their position in life. Sound familiar? If everyone in modern times embraced the fact that each of us holds the power to change our position in life, would we be as passionate about giving our time and money to a candidate who promises to do basically what the ancient alchemist did?

This isn't to say that you shouldn't lobby for causes you believe in. Instead, I advocate self-reliance, a trait that can be nurtured in everyone. If you want something in life, your best chance at attaining it is to push for it locally, starting with yourself. That way, much like the first domino, you are taking control of the only thing you know you really have control over: yourself at this moment.

As stated earlier, it is a very human characteristic to look for help from an outside source because it shifts the responsibility to affect change from self to other. Unfortunately, it also takes the power to do so with it. When it comes to modern-day politics, much like the modern media, with which it has been grossly intertwined, the real problem lies in the idea that so much of what politicians do is monetarily motivated and the well-being of constituents is typically an afterthought.

You may believe that your representative is different. I'll humor you for a second and say that he or she is. Have you ever written a letter to your representative for something? Petitioning government is a lengthy, if not exhaustive, process to effect change. Relying on bureaucracy to solve the problems of an individual is, at best, poor problem-solving. At worst, it's thievery, as precious time is wasted and thrown into the tiller of inefficiency.

Consider this example. One of my biggest issues with the government is their massive subsidization of the corn industry; thus, sugar, in the form of high-fructose corn syrup, ends up in an alarmingly large amount of the food that makes up the standard American diet. For this reason, many people are addicted to something they can't see. All they recognize is their compulsion for more. They are in a prison so complete that they have convinced themselves they are free.

For me to be angry with the Food and Drug Administration over this matter takes time and energy out of my life, not theirs. My best course of action to effect change is to cut sugar out of my life altogether. Though it is much more difficult than filling out a form or writing a letter, it is starting as locally as possible (with myself). This first step of starting local is crucial and should not be overlooked. Many people end up frustrated when they are unable to change the world, but the truth is, their words are powerless because they are unable to change their own world. When your actions are aligned with what you profess, you have immense power. When they are not, you are limited to hollow words and frustration. (Those people tend to raise their voice rather than strengthen their argument.)

From this point, *if* I can succeed at embodying my own desires, I can educate others to do the same via my written and spoken message. Creating these types of messages are activities that energize me. I love doing them, and because I love doing them, I continuously improve my craft and get better at them. This allows me to reach more people organically, as people tend to share a message that resonates with them. The more people I reach, the more lives I can change for the better. The result is that I not only affect my life and others' lives, but I am immensely satisfied while doing it. The bonus is that I don't care what any politician might have to say about this issue and I spend zero time yelling at the television. You can bang your head against that wall as long as you want, but you shouldn't fool yourself into thinking it's going to change anything. Consider abstaining from modern alchemy. Consider voting for yourself.

As we manage the small details and the seemingly mundane aspects of our lives, we see that being overly cautious about everything we consume is part of that process. The adage that what we consume begins to consume us is all too true in today's world. Your mind is one of the most precious resources you have, but it is not made of steel. Your mind will form and adapt just like any other muscle.

Though self-love is often understood as what you give to yourself, it might be helpful to see that it is also expressed as what you keep *from* yourself. A standard for what we allow to affect our thought process not only ensures that we don't end up as a puppet for poor ideas, but it also teaches the world how to interact with us in a way that allows us to show up as the best version of ourselves. It's what they call a win-win scenario.

Find your normal

Many times, I have gotten out of work on Friday, driven for hours into the mountains, and slept in my car. I'll wake up at five or six o'clock in the morning, and I'll spend the next twelve to thirty hours running in those same mountains. Then I'll get back in my car, drive home, sleep for a few hours, and go back to work on Monday. I'll be a bit worse for wear, with a bit of a gangster lean when I walk because of blisters and sore muscles, but I'll be happy.

Writing this behavior off as erratic might be easy, an isolated incident of insanity that allows you to protect your conception of normal, but you should know I am not alone on these adventures. In fact, most of the races are sold out. Every weekend, thousands of us are out there testing ourselves. We test not only our physical abilities but also our resolve and ability to endure as we flirt with the limits of our bodies' capabilities.

Many people will spend that exact same time gobbling up happy-hour specials and repetitive errand-running. To me, this sounds like a death sentence. One of my biggest fears in this world is that every single day will not be able to be differentiated from the one before. This, however, is the life that most people accept as "normal." I don't say this to disparage the routine but to let you know that there's an entire other world out there if you feel so inclined to explore it.

The fact is, a weekend jaunt like this has now become pretty standard. At first, it seemed like a lot, but my baseline is always adjusting and keeping pace with my aspirations. That is the beauty of growth. As you begin to grow comfortable in something that was originally uncomfortable, you are gifted with more capacity. This is what it means to level up, and it is exactly how you go from running a five-kilometer race to a hundred-kilometer race. Of course, the idea of running for multiple hours seems scary at first, but this is not because running for hours is not doable. Running for hours is scary only when you have not yet learned to dance with your limitations. You haven't expanded your horizons, and as a result, you don't know the version of you that sits on the other side of them. This works for your mind and your physical abilities, and it is the key to growth as a person. You may replace running with anything in this life you feel drawn to. It all has a horizon, and it all calls you at your depth to go explore. Every single experience that introduces a new variable to an old thought pattern forces you to run, evolve, or, in most cases, both.

Adapting to the unknown

If you do not bring forth what is within you, what you do not bring forth will destroy you."
—Gospel of Thomas

I had gone to Hawaii to visit family during my junior year of high school, and after I had gotten a little taste of the world outside my small hometown in Maine, I knew without a doubt I would have to experience it. When I graduated high school, my first move was to

Florida for college. While, admittedly, I was a bit nervous, overall, I couldn't have been more excited to get out on my own. The problem was that I still possessed thought patterns from my small town.

My psyche did not take exposure to the wider world well. I badly wanted to experience the world, but the big world was all very new and had an intimidating and foreign culture I had never experienced. I didn't know how to adjust. What I should have met with open arms, I met with frustration. I found myself angry when I was exposed to an overwhelming number of opinions that were different from my own. Ironically, this was what I had wanted and was one reason I had left home in the first place. So, what did I do? The only thing I felt like I could do: I packed up my life, started dating my high school girlfriend again, and moved back home for the life I had never wanted.

This is the reality for many of us. Stuck between who we want to be and who we feel comfortable being, we retreat into a lesser version of ourselves. Eventually, though, our depth will come calling again. The soul will not settle as easily as we will.

After a few more bouts with college, a few more break-ups with the same person, and only a few months at home, I realized I was not going to be happy in a life of perpetually settling. At this point, I did the next logical thing I could think of and drove to the Navy office to sign up for the military on my lunch break. I called out for the rest of the workday and spent it taking physical exams and trying to qualify for a job that sounded interesting. Nine days later, I got on a bus to leave my hometown for the final time.

Of course, I experienced the same culture shock as the first time I had left, if not markedly worse, but this time, I couldn't go anywhere. Contracts are a good move on the part of the military because, without them, the military would have about six employees after the first couple of months. Being exposed to new ideas and thoughts leaves you with two options: run or evolve. This time, since running was taken off the table, I reluctantly chose to evolve. I realized within a year that many of the beliefs I held were flat-out wrong, ignorant, or really didn't resonate with me as a person. And this was only a small percent of the real evolution I would eventually experience.

Being exposed to ideas with which you aren't familiar is the beauty of leaving your hometown, no matter where it is. People often feel like they are constrained by where their parents raised them. This would make total sense if you were a tree. The leaves and seeds fall off of trees and can only go so far. For humans, though, I have found that acting like a tree in this sense is a terrible survival mechanism. We will grow to resent roots we did not ask for or want in the first place. Where you end up isn't so important, especially at first. The important part is acknowledging the part of yourself that simply cannot stand not knowing what lies on the other side of your ambitions.

Mind expansion like this can also be accomplished by reading books that are the polar opposite of what you believe to be right. You might find that the other half has better ideas than you thought. You also might find that what other people consider normal is different than what you do. From there, it isn't long until the idea of normalcy disintegrates altogether.

Breaking average

"I would rather die of thirst than drink from the cup of mediocrity."
– graffiti written on a bar wall in Bahrain, circa 2007

For something that so rigidly controls human existence, reality is the most malleable set of guidelines. This is because your idea of reality is typically the culmination of everything that has influenced you from the moment you were born. People are generally willing to settle for a life that is less than exemplary because they view the reality they've been handed as something that cannot be manipulated. Average, normal, and the status quo are all based on at least some ideas that are not your own.

The definition of "average" depends on comparison to something else; therefore, to break average, you have to be willing to let go of the idea of defining success in any sort of relative manner. Five is only average in the presence of a six and a four. We are addicted to comparing our lives to those of the people we perceive as better, and social media has succeeded in its ability to magnify this need. If you are going to find any kind of lasting happiness in this life, it will be when you are awakened to the fact that your journey is yours alone. Sure, there will be people who will help you out along the way and others who seem to get in the way, but true success can only be found in the pursuit of an ideal that you alone have deemed worthy. It is about your values, your actions, and whether or not those two things are in alignment.

Define and conquer

When it comes to self-improvement, two types of people exist: those who are eager and those who are indifferent. Some may appear to be outwardly objective to it, but once you see past their preconceived notions about what the words mean, that resistant exterior is revealed as a guise. No one is actively engaged in ensuring they are not progressing as humans, at least, not on purpose.

I am going to assume, because you are this far into a book dedicated to helping you achieve more in life, that you fall into camp with the former. Your goal is to maximize the human experience. You may not have phrased it like that in the past. You may not have admitted it out loud, but that's why we do anything, right? That's why we read and learn and why we work harder and hope to make more money. That's what gets us up early when sleep is so much easier. You may not even have the thought of self-improvement or personal development at the front of your mind when you are contending with your life, but deep down, when you strip away everything else, the goal is to maximize this human experience by maximizing your ability *to* experience. This is one reason why we beat ourselves up so badly when we fall short of our own ideal. Making the most of this one chance at life is what it often comes down to.

As a species, we are transitioning, and growth is not optional. You can hold onto your transistor radio and keep your mind as closed as you'd like, but the future is coming. Technology is revolutionizing the work we do.

In some cases, technology is replacing the work we have known in the past, like manufacturing and low-wage services. Artificial intelligence is on the brink of explosion. As much a knuckle-dragger like myself hates to admit it, the world as a whole needs brute strength less and less. Every day, the world is becoming much more accustomed to the gentle hands and sharp mind of the coder.

Taking all of this into account, the transition isn't complete. Our biology cannot evolve as fast as technology presents itself. This is true with the food we eat as much as it is the jobs we do. Both the human spirit and genome are still reliant on many of the artifacts that have been chiseled and fashioned over millions of years of evolution. In light of this, we must embrace the future with trepidation. We must assimilate while keeping in mind the differences between the machines we use and the humans who operate them. The differences are still stark.

Chapter 4. Confusing Comfort for Happiness

"The more voluntary suffering you build into your life,
the less involuntary suffering will affect your life."
—Tim Ferriss

I had just turned nineteen years old, and I was locked in a cement-walled cell. I was naked and sitting on a cold floor made of dirty cement. I hadn't slept in three or four days, and I hadn't eaten in even more. I was past hunger, headaches, and even pain. Pain, I have found, breaks a lot sooner than we do. Think about it like a new filling in your tooth. At first, the newly exposed nerves can hurt at the slightest sense of anything too warm or cold. Over time, those nerves dull and stop firing, and the pain slowly subsides. In any case, the pain was gone, and I was essentially numb to the outside world.

I would slowly begin drifting off into sleep-induced nothingness just in time for the guard to come by and bang on my cell door. The guard expected a prompt response of, "War criminal five-four," from me. In comparison to the previous few days, it was kind of nice being in the cell. I could have done without the sound of a baby crying, blasted from a speaker above me on a fifteen-second loop, but other than the noise, I wasn't being harassed or waterboarded, and no one was grilling me about my religion, so all in all, the night in the cell was a bit of a welcome break.

I'm lucky in the way that almost all Americans are lucky. I wasn't an actual prisoner of war. I wasn't even subject to war. I was just training. I had joined the Navy a few months before, and due to the way things worked out with my training pipeline, Survive Evade Resist Escape (SERE) school was my first real test after boot camp. I vividly remember only one real thought: *I have fucked up a lot in my life, but joining the Navy is a whole new level of fucked up.* I wasn't eased out of my comfort zone; I was torn out of it, and I reeled to get my bearings. I had been taken from my hometown of parties and chasing girls and placed in the deepest depths of suffering. Well, an imitation of the depths, anyway. Either way, I was going through something altogether different than I was used to, and the contrast was painful.

When the school was over, I went back to Coronado, California, to begin the next school. Well, that's not exactly true. I went through the mandatory psychiatric evaluation. Then I went to McDonald's, where I promptly ate forty-seven dollars worth of greasy, amazing food. And then I threw up. And then I realized something incredible about life.

Upon climbing into my bed back in the barracks, which, I assure you, was no Tempur-Pedic, I experienced joy like never before. I felt pure heaven in the comfort of a terribly mass-produced bed in a room with zero amenities and no television. It was unlike anything I had ever experienced, and I realized something that has become a recurring theme of my life and this book: true joy and happiness are only possible in contrast to the opposite. The deeper we go into the pain cave, the more amazement we feel with daily life. Had I gone straight from my life after high school to that barracks room, I would have been miserable, but because I made a pit stop in hell first, my frame of reference was drastically shifted, and as a result, I found happiness like I hadn't previously known.

You don't have to go through military training, and you don't have to lose seventeen pounds in two weeks from starvation, but you can and should learn from the example. There is much more enjoyment in a life of overcoming obstacles than of avoiding them. Every so often, you should create obstacles, as you are lucky enough to have the ability to overcome them. Over time, you might even learn how to thrive when faced with them.

In the end, you won't remember the chores you did around the house or the endless days you sat in the office. You will remember the mountains you conquered and the ones that nearly conquered you. You will remember fighting through experiences, and you will remember the times that hurt so much the hurting stopped.

There is no scenario in life that allows one to escape pain in any permanent sense. Temporary relief is a minor disruption to an otherwise inevitable life of one pain point after another. The first noble truth of Buddhism points out that all of life is ultimately *dukkha*, unquenchable suffering.

A heart attack, from what I hear, is a painful experience. On the other hand, reducing the risk of heart attack isn't without its pain, either. Constantly getting yourself to the gym, enduring the pain of discipline when it comes to making good diet choices, and avoiding fast food might be considered painful. Even for the most motivated of individuals, getting the lifestyle aspect right from a health standpoint is certainly not without its pain points. Regardless of your path, you are going to undergo a certain amount of pain while trying to stay healthy; you just have to decide which type of pain is worth enduring.

The same goes for almost any scenario in life. Starting a business is an excruciatingly difficult experience. Early mornings, late nights, and stress levels through the roof are not easy things to manage. On the other hand, going to work for someone else, rearranging your life according to someone else's schedule, and knowing your paycheck is largely in the hands of someone else are also points of frustration. To an entrepreneur, these are unbearable facts. Your tolerance for risk and what you consider to be the makings of a good life will influence which of these pains you are willing to endure, but the fact of suffering will remain.

On a recent ski trip, I noticed a bartender who was waiting on me had slipped into the back room and taken a Percocet. Apparently, his knees ached from making his way from one end of the bar to the other for a six-hour shift. A life of comfort may feel good at first, but that only lasts long enough to allow the pain to change forms, prolonging the misery. Often, we incur acute pain in the second half of our life due to ease in the first half. Alas, none of us will ever truly escape pain.

The goal, then, should be to pursue pain in life, pain that is useful and allows you to experience this world on your own terms. People love to point out the hours I spend in the gym or on the trails and tell me how I will assuredly need this surgery or that repair or how so much running "can't be good for you." To this, I reply, "I am simply choosing to confront life's inevitable pain on my own terms." I choose six hours of moving through the mountains, powered by grit, over six hours in the bar, powered by Percocet.

Pick your poison

"My wife and I don't go to cocktail parties. We run ultra-marathons. That way we get to be around genuine people without all of the bullsh*t."
–Random guy who gave me a Red Bull when I was twenty-seven hours into running a race.

The military is notorious for the bond created amongst soldiers. This isn't because the military only recruits from a certain demographic. In fact, that couldn't be further from the truth. The first day I arrived at boot camp, I looked around and had never seen so many different shades of people gathered in one space.

Realistically, any bond that would be built on anything superficial, like skin color or social class, is nothing compared to the comradery built in the military.

Many people have speculated about what causes such a kinship as they strive to build it into their own company or organization. I'm here to tell you it is not complicated. The camaraderie built in the armed forces stems from two things: shared values and the hardship endured in pursuit of those values. Something in the human spirit is awakened when resolve is summoned. It teases things out of us, things we did not even know we had.

Difficult times, not to mention life-threatening times, cut through all of the trivial exteriors of life. People come to grips with their own vulnerability, their reliance on others, and the fact that their internal drive may be all they have to get them through. These are things that the comfort of your couch can never give you.

One of my favorite things about ultra-marathon running, and one of the reasons I have become so addicted to daunting challenges, is that beyond pain and suffering lies a beautiful rawness that most people will never get to experience. When you push on for long enough, the pain will eventually go away, leaving your conscious mind. Once the pain leaves your mind, however, it will sit below the surface, carving away at the layers of the mask you've learned to wear. Persevere for long enough, and there will be nothing at all that stands between you and the world. This vulnerability will terrify and exhilarate you as you begin to meet the person you are below the person you believe yourself to be.

All my life, I've suffered, as many men in the West do, lost in a land of misunderstanding as I struggled to connect how I was feeling with what was happening around and to me. I eventually wrote myself off as somewhat emotionless and stopped trying to understand what I clearly did not have.

Then I came through the mile-fifty aid station at the Santa Barbara hundred-mile foot race after running all night long. A friend asked me how I was doing, and I promptly started crying as I told her I was fine. Oddly enough, I was fine. But I was also crying, something I had only experienced about once a year for the last decade. Something new in me was coming forward as my commitment to forward progress on foot revealed layers to my depth that I never knew that I had. Once you know how to access a place emotionally, going back becomes easier, and over time, who you are is expanded. Slowly but surely, you experience the world in a completely different way.

This is why I can tell you with confidence that I do not love the pain. I simply put up with the pain because I'm interested in meeting the person I am on the other side of it, the person capable of outlasting it. When confronting pain in the future, he'll be a good reference point to have.

Into the night

At nineteen years old, I struggled to find my footing between the recklessness of the teenage years and the maturity of adulthood. I didn't know where I fit in, and I found it easy to dwell on the sadness of not belonging. I was in that special time of life where you are old enough to die for your country but not old enough to buy a beer. Many of my friends seemed to know exactly what they wanted, but I was hungry for life and had no idea which direction to go. At the time, this felt a lot like depression, though now I see it was mostly rooted in a lack of perspective.

Getting stuck inside your own head and allowing negative thoughts to consume you are easy when you are alone on your couch, and if you don't make a move quickly, this is also where real depression can begin to set in. That is when I discovered something that would lay the groundwork for a much better life. One night, as I sat with my own struggle, I put on my running shoes and hit the road. Thinking back, I am not sure I even closed the door behind me. With no plan, I began running. Other than school sports, I had never really run for the sake of it, so this was where it all really began. For the first time in a long time, I didn't give a damn where I ended up. I put one foot in front of the other until my knees and legs hurt, and then I kept running. I ran through the entire playlist on my iPod Shuffle three times.

I couldn't tell you how long I actually ran, but something in me refused to turn around. Way past safe and comfortable, I just kept trekking into the night, into exhaustion, into my own psyche. Finally, deep into the night, when everything below my waist hurt more than I had ever known it could, I stopped and looked around. I was sore and lost, with no money, so I did the only thing I could do: I put one foot in front of the other and started to dig myself out of the hole. Eventually, early the next morning, I knew I would get back home. Truthfully, I might not have had I not run into scared family members who had been out driving around, looking for me after getting worried when I hadn't returned home for dinner.

That night, I woke in fits of cramped legs and feelings of perpetual motion. Five days passed before I could walk up or down stairs with any sort of efficiency. The small things that had me stressed out seemed to fall away into the night with every step and every barrier I ran through. People may not advise running as far as you can in one direction with no plan to get home, but honestly, those people don't understand this sort of solution. Sometimes getting yourself in too deep is the only real way to find out what you are made of. And once you see what you're truly made of, the inconsequential things begin to fade.

The give and take of consumer culture

Any entrepreneur worth their salt will tell you that the reason a business exists is to solve a problem or serve a need in the world. We have progressed to the point where many needs are not only met but available to us at affordable prices. The result is that luxuries are available to more and more people regardless of their social class.

Consider Amazon Fresh, the service that delivers groceries to you based on your selection from an app on your phone. The implications of this shouldn't be lost on you. Thousands of years ago, acquiring food was significantly more complicated. From what I hear, hunting down a predatory animal with a homemade weapon was quite tough. We have progressed so far as a society that an act of life and death can now be accomplished without ever leaving your couch or interrupting the Kardashians.

While this is a true testament to how amazing this society we have built really is, it is also a reason for trepidation. When that much comfort lies at the touch of a button, so does the probability of a less-than-stellar existence. Comfort seeps into every corner of life, and as it does, the animal in us loses track of what it's doing here.

Many things are available to us so quickly that good, old-fashioned delayed gratification has become a thing of the past. Food is fast, answers are fast (Google), and entertainment is on demand. Unfortunately, one of the inalienable laws of life is that anything worth having takes time to get. Being great at something takes repetition; building real wealth is acquired over time when many good financial decisions are made in succession, and life tends to reward those who are patient.

Delaying gratification and choosing the more difficult road from time to time make the actual comforts of life much more comfortable. Go camping and sleep under the stars for a few days. While the fresh air and connection to nature feel great, the return to your bed also feels so much better than you remember. That contrast gives us the opportunity to appreciate the great things we have in life that are right in front of us. Comfort for comfort's sake breeds boredom. Comfort in the face of adversity breeds appreciation and gratitude.

Life beyond comfort

Have you ever been riding your bike on the road and had someone honk at you as they angrily swerved around you? Apparently, the inconvenience of them moving their hands two feet to the left and then two feet back to the right on the steering wheel to swerve around you was just too much for them to bear. As Joe De Sena, founder of the Spartan Race and the Death Race, would say, that driver is someone who needs to recalibrate their frame of reference.

Just like it is easy for us to get stuck in our own heads and grow depressed if we don't figure out a way to get a little perspective, it is also easy for us to be misguided when it comes to hardship. The fact that we have become so entitled that a verbal lashing seems the best way to deal with driving around someone biking on the road speaks volumes about the state of our culture. When we get used to a lifestyle that is completely free of discomfort, we lack the correct perspective on real discomfort, and we look like a dick.

When it comes to shifting perspective, I am personally biased toward physical movement, as it provides the exact shift necessary and is typically very cost-effective. One hundred burpees every morning costs you nothing but sweat, but the payoff of an elevated mood, being a better person to be around, and having a view of life that ensures menial tasks remain menial is worth a lot. How much better would you be at work if you got all your suffering done at the beginning of the day, ensuring the problems that arise pale in comparison?

Exposing yourself to pain radically forces you to get your priorities straight and helps your mind separate what matters from what most assuredly does not. In that sense, it acts much the same as hindsight in that it clears everything up. Most importantly, it gives you the contrast necessary for happiness. Without it, you are destined to wind up in a purgatory where you feel neither hurt nor elation. Emptiness pulls at our souls and transforms the vibrant colors that are meant to be life into a shade of gray that is rarely worth experiencing.

The relativity of pain

To deal with pain and make it work for you, first look at it for what it is: pain is immediate informational feedback to a problem. Thus, being delivered from that feedback prematurely does not actually solve the problem; it merely covers it up for a period of time. If you take a cough suppressant when you have a head cold, it might be fine. If you take it when you have lung cancer, it may prolong your ability to know what to do. Pain, like most things in life, is neutral. It's value is based solely on the value system you bring to it.

The lottery teaches us what happens when you are prematurely delivered from stress. The National Endowment for Financial Education has found that roughly seventy percent of all lottery winners or people who get a large sum of money from a big windfall end up broke or bankrupt shortly after. They don't understand money, that is, the principles of economics that allow a person to keep it and make more of it. In contrast, many stories of self-made millionaires who lose their entire fortune only to gain it all again are out there. The answer to any problem isn't to hope that someone will solve it, but to sit with it and try to find out what it is trying to tell you.

When you are buried by troubles, the answer is to grab whatever happens to be next to you, a spoon if it's all that you have, and begin digging your way out. The answer is not being trouble-free but learning how to become someone who can work through their troubles. That's the part of this experience that you'll bring with you and apply to the next pain point you find yourself in.

A final note on pain

Most people concede that discomfort is key in the growth process. What I've found, however, is that most people acknowledge that without realizing that they only like to be uncomfortable in ways they are comfortable being. For example, I am comfortable putting my body through all-out hell in an ultramarathon all day long, sometimes for days on end. As I said earlier, though, sitting with my emotions feels a lot like

I'm steeped in boiling water. Some people find getting to the gym every day at 5:00 am to be much more comfortable than not going. Not going may bring up all sorts of unresolved body issues.

Here we see that regardless of our own comfort zone, the key to our growth always lies outside it. Life, then, is a series of never-ending evolutions. If we have the courage to continuously brave the edges of our own bubble wrap, we find that our evolution supports the growth of our soul and who we are here to be. If we resist that edge, we do keep evolving, but we have little say in where to. Some will find that a life of shrinking back from their fear of the unknown and the uncomfortable will force their evolution into a place where the entire world closes in around them. As fear begets more fear, their psyche shrinks and loses the ability to contend with the stress.

Chapter 5. The Truth about Success

"He has achieved success who has lived well, laughed often, and loved much;
Who has enjoyed the trust of pure women, the respect of intelligent men and the love of little children;
Who has filled his niche and accomplished his task;
Who has never lacked appreciation of Earth's beauty or failed to express it;
Who has left the world better than he found it,
Whether an improved poppy, a perfect poem, or a rescued soul;
Who has always looked for the best in others and given them the best he had;
Whose life was an inspiration;
Whose memory a benediction."
— Bessie Anderson Stanley

There is no road map that tells us how someone might become successful in life. The path to success is not linear; it's more like a pretzel taped to a hockey stick. We twist and turn our way through setbacks, lessons we repeat because we did not learn, and roads that just come to an end for no apparent reason—perhaps the market crumbles, a relationship ends, or a new, better product launches with more success, and the competition capitalize on the trend. It can be years before we get to the part that propels us upward, free and clear of early setbacks and obstacles.

Those who do figure out how to succeed in any given area of life, however, tend to know how to replicate this success. This is partly why you see millionaires lose everything, only to gain it all back again. They understand what matters beyond what everyone else understands. They see the underlying systems that are in place and they work off of those. They also tend to understand what within themselves holds them back from what they want. This concerns the way they talk to themselves, the way they think about their projects, and their general mindset and ability to actually allow themselves to have the success they seek. Most of us who never escape the pretzel have some deep-seated belief that we don not actually deserve to.

It's also important to understand that just because someone has gained success for themselves in a given area, this success doesn't indicate they have the ability to teach you how to achieve those same results. I see this often in the fitness world I began my career in. The fact that doing something and teaching something are actually very different disciplines is lost on many of today's self-improvement gurus. Coaching and mentoring are skill sets in and of themselves.

It is also worth noting that the self-help/personal development industry, which may promise you success, is crawling with scam artists who are less than genuine about helping you. Beware the moment anyone talks to you as if you are a number and not a person. Beware when someone tells you how much they know more than they ask you what you need. Beware when they project their value system onto you (this may look like them defining success for the partnership without your say).

Collaboration is also a massive part of the success journey. In effect, collaboration is how we become more than ourselves. When it comes to considering partnering with others, pay special attention to how they talk about their clients and customers when they are not around. People who see things instead of people might know how to find shortsighted material success but living within their own soul will be hell before too long, and they'll start to look to the person next to them to pull them out of that hell. It's not your job to drown with people who hate themselves or others.

One unique aspect of existing at the far end of a long chain of unbroken evolution is that we are standing on the shoulders of giants. The success of others leaves clues that can help us navigate the myriad of struggles we'll find ourselves in. If you look in the right places, those clues begin to present themselves. Don't look at people for what they've achieved; look at them for methods. Look at them for inner peace. Look at them for guidance and not replication.

We can look at many different methods of obtaining success and know with some certainty whether certain factors played a role. For these factors to be considered, they must arise from an aggregate of many successful people; this way, we can avoid the one-off quirks of some. If you put success habits into a Venn diagram, our focus is on the factors shared by the many. Once we identify the shared principles, they begin to build a framework that we can look for success within. This is a far more efficient way to go about the daunting task of finding success. Consider each piece of advice as part of your framework, scaffolding meant to assist your climb.

The first step to getting anywhere is, of course, knowing where you currently are. Often, instead of facing our discomfort or resentment about the way our life is going, we tell ourselves that we are happy or that we should be - until we begin to believe it. Over time, we will have habitualized these lies, and if we aren't careful, we'll do this with every aspect of our lives. This is often how we end up apathetic but not sure why. We have everything we should want, and we don't know where our disdain lies. Often it lies in the lies that lie outside our awareness, because we have spent so much time dismissing them.

This is the act formally known as settling. Truthfully, we should refer to it as deferment because, in reality, deferring is all you are doing. You're delaying disappointment to a later date, hoping that eventually contentment will take its place. It won't. You cannot grow from delusion.

Whatever you are "settling" for will surely resurface later when you can no longer keep it effectively repressed. What do you tell yourself, your spouse, or your friends that, below the surface, you know isn't really acceptable to you? How much of yourself are you compromising by settling? Of course, any relationship calls for a certain level of compromise to work effectively, but the real question is, what compromises have you made that are gradually eating at your soul? It's best to address those things before they manifest as physical illness or a mid-life crisis.

The world isn't against you; people are just out for themselves

When you are starting out, it may feel like the world is conspiring against you. It may feel like you can't catch a break, and, because of this, success eludes you. The truth, however, is far more difficult to stomach. In most cases, we are positioned against ourselves, and we are projecting that onto the world around us. Of course things do not always work out. Of course momentum is hard to get when you have none. If you live in this way, it will feel as if everything is against you; even though failure is teaching you what won't work, setbacks are teaching you how to optimize your approach, and lessons are buried in everything, whether they work out or not. What's interesting is that if you can find it within yourself to think abundantly, to look at problems as opportunities for growth and the universe as being generally for you, you will eventually find that the world is happy to go along with that story as well. It can help to realize that life, in general, isn't about what happens to you but how you choose to react to what happens to you.

As you begin to try to accomplish more and more in life, you will inevitably start hitting walls that feel like they are meant to stop you. I like to think about these walls and obstacles as gatekeepers meant to reserve the best parts of life for those willing to put in the work and figure out the equation. Gatekeepers are guardians of the standard, ensuring that only the deserving reach the promised land. Thinking in this way can be beneficial if you are the sort who is prone to rising to challenges.

Rather than put yourself within a story of achievement, you might also think analytically about the situation. We place value on commodities that are rare. Typically, the rarer they are, the more value we place on them. This is why the things in life that have become the most sought after and synonymous with success have also turned out to be the most difficult to obtain. The rarity is what makes them so.

However you conceptualize your problem, it may feel as if others are conspiring against you. It can be helpful to understand that we are all simply doing what we think we must to survive. Very few people are against you; they are simply looking out for themselves.

I cannot stress strongly enough the importance of ridding yourself of the scarcity mentality. The scarcity mentality will limit your potential in every aspect of life. It can be easy to start believing you need to guard your ideas and protect your little sphere of importance, but nothing could be further from the truth. Nowhere is this more relevant or evident than in entrepreneurship.

Have you ever heard anyone say that they have a good idea for a business? The very next words normally are, "But you have to promise not to tell anyone." Guess what? Everyone has a good idea. In fact, most of us have hundreds of good ideas in any given year. It is the execution of any idea that matters, and any business owner who has achieved anything will tell you the same thing. Anyone who would even consider executing your idea is a doer, and they are already too busy executing their own ideas.

Instead, look to share your ideas with everyone. Engage in deep conversation about ideas, projects, and anything else that lights you up. Build on those ideas and look for feedback. At the very least, your ideas will improve just by fleshing them out. This is an abundance mentality. This is the mindset of thought leaders and great thinkers everywhere. We should not act like money, success, and potential are finite. The only thing that is finite is your time, and it is being wasted every moment you hoard your thoughts, ideas, and gifts.

When I first began my business, it felt like the world was rooting for my demise. This isn't a rare occurrence. Government workers rarely care about your business when they are collecting taxes and imposing regulations. Subcontractors are trying to maximize profit as you look to squeeze profit out from between them and your customer. Retailers are rarely sympathetic as they slash the prices of your product and move it off of their shelves. Manufacturers have no problem collecting down payments on a quote and then charging you for overrun in cost. The post office will delay or lose your shipment from time to time, and all the customer knows is that you didn't deliver. I could go on, but you get the point.

Again, very few people are going out of their way to screw you over; they are all just looking out for themselves and for their own livelihoods. Government workers, contractors, retailers, and manufacturers, all must pay for their lives, too. They all have their own long line of people who are making their lives significantly more difficult. Being sympathetic to that fact in all of your interactions will help you give the same thing to yourself when you let someone down. Which, of course, you will.

You get what you accept

Generally speaking, life is a direct reflection of two things: what you expect and what you accept. To my mind, this concept opens up a conversation about self-love. We often see the narrative that self-love is self-acceptance and acceptance should be applied to everything. To this, I would reply, that's not love. Love has an inherent element of truth in it. You can accept yourself and also hold yourself accountable to the truth that will serve you. Just like we must have standards for what we allow to penetrate into our consciousness, we should do the same for every aspect of our lives. We call these boundaries, and they provide a way of letting the world know how to interact with us. They preserve our world and, simultaneously, our best selves *for* the world. Boundaries teach the world what we expect and what we will accept.

The secret is that you will often get what you expect. That goes for results anywhere in life: relationships, business, etc. This doesn't mean you can get whatever you want simply because you expect it. You first have to learn how to stop accepting less than that expectation, which, depending on how you think about yourself, can be quite difficult. Either way, you'll find the world has a way of catering to belief.

The quickest way to end up in an unhappy relationship and with a dissatisfying life is to generally not believe you deserve more. When you are on the outside of a situation like this, you see it easily. That's one reason you might have a friend in an abusive relationship who stays even though you can clearly see it is to their detriment. It's also the same reason you may end up as that friend while your loved ones all tell you consistently that you deserve better. What we expect and accept often makes up the lens that we are looking through, so it is difficult to see if it could or should be more.

One sure way to begin becoming aware of your expectations is by taking the uncomfortable step of reevaluating your life and being honest with what you find. Regularly step back and try to objectively look at where you are and the results you are getting. Ask yourself if what you are getting is the best possible outcome, and if it isn't, then ask yourself why. How are you contributing to your own lack of fulfillment or success? Are you doing something you know you shouldn't be or not doing something you know you should? What are you allowing that are causing dissatisfaction? It might be time to shake things up. You should never be afraid to change things. Chances are good that there are at least a few areas in your life where it is time to level up.

EQ > IQ

EQ is your emotional quotient, while IQ is your intelligence quotient. IQ gets a lot of focus and press because it is broadly associated with success in every area of life. The problem for our purposes, though, is that it is largely fixed. You can take care of yourself, you can take supplements that enhance cognitive function, and you can commit to a healthy movement practice, all of which will increase your IQ. And though you should do all of these things if maximizing potential is a value of yours, you should know that the effects are minimal.

On the other hand, you can ALWAYS become more self-aware, and there is no limit to that. You can become aware of how you show up and make people feel. You can learn to articulate how you actually feel and how that affects how you show up. You can become aware of your subconscious compulsions and drives toward self-sabotage and work through them. You can leverage self-awareness and awareness of others to get things done that genius cannot.

We are very clearly social animals, so understanding this aspect of ourselves and that it can be improved is a sure way of helping you navigate the success minefield with less friction. Your emotional intelligence is your ability to read a situation or an interaction. It is not simply relating to others, but also includes posture, nonverbal cues, and all other indicators of mood and mindset.

Hard skills are your ability to do your job well. Mastering these, whatever they might be for your profession, will allow you to charge more and increase your billable hours. Soft skills like trustworthiness and likability allow you to turn a game of golf into an account that pays you for years to come. While a place always exists for a skilled tactician, it can't be the end game if you want to maximize opportunity. People only hand money and opportunities over to people they know, like, and trust, and you have the ability to work hard at being one of those people. People with hard skills are often replaceable. I can teach you to use Microsoft Office, but it will take me far longer to teach you how to be a good leader, garner confidence from others, and be someone other people actually want to work with. If it's down to choice, most people will choose the person they relate to.

Invest in yourself

I have found that people are often reluctant to go after the life they want because they are hiding behind the fact that too much risk is involved in pursuing it. Typically, the actual risk involved in an activity is less than what a person perceives, especially compared to the so-called "safe investments" we are taught to put our money into.

For example, look at the stock market. In a nutshell, the stock market works something like this: individual companies are all registered with the market in which investors invest. When you buy stock in those companies, you are essentially investing in them and their leadership. They are getting your money, and in return, you get a percentage ownership in their company, giving you the ability to share in their profits if they have any. When they are conducting business so that profits are high, the stock price goes up—that is, your initial investment grows. Over time, a consistent return on investment (ROI) of eight to twelve percent has spread out among the stock market as a whole. That is the collective return of all the different companies.

A mutual fund is a collection of different companies meant to help you spread out your risk. The best performers get an eight to twelve percent ROI, mirroring the market. This makes it a good vehicle over a long period of time because you are protected against the failure of any company. Investment in mutual funds is touted as more of a retirement move. However, this does not account for the problem of a downturn in the market.

Even if you played the "safe odds" and invested your savings in many different mutual funds over a long time, you were screwed if you were ready to retire in 2007—or in 1819, 1837, 1857, 1869, 1893, 1896, 1901, 1907, 1929, 1937, 1962, 1987,1989, and 1990 because these years also saw panics in the market that caused a downturn and huge loss of funds. Now, the chances of you being ready to cash in at that exact same time aren't astronomical, but it could and has happened to millions.

In 2007, people bet on the government being able to regulate the market and protect investors. They bet on the CEOs of corporations making good decisions. They trusted financial advisors with a fiduciary responsibility to give sound financial advice. What happened? Few of these entities came through on their ends of the bargain, and people set to retire in 2007 had to work an extra three to four years, hoping that the market turned around so they could cash out. In essence, they hoped that the same sets of people who had failed to do what they were supposed to do would change and do their jobs so they could cash in on decades of hard work and diligent saving.

Maybe you weren't ready to retire then, and maybe you have a long time before you actually can or want to retire. Are you willing to gamble with your future? I was working closely with the financial industry around that time, and I saw a lot of scared and helpless people who suddenly realized they had bet on the wrong person. Of course, the price eventually came back up as the market recovered, but whose timeline are you living on? Please hear me correctly on this: investment in others is a good idea; it's just not the *only* idea. You are also a worthy investment.

Spend money for things that are going to increase your own ability to make money. Seminars, classes, books, retreats, and networking events meant to make you more marketable will always be a safe bet because you retain the power to decide what should happen next. People who understood money prospered during all of these same moments.

Creativity > Resources

In the twenty-first century, we no longer need to bend to the will of the beaten path, because we have the technology to skirt around it. That is the beauty of our world. Singers have blown up and made a living doing what they love, not by getting record deals and dealing with corporations but by having a unique sound and building a following on Instagram and YouTube.

Authors, personalities, and entrepreneurs have done the same thing.

I once convinced the Navy to pay me to compete in a two-day adventure race because I put a report together showing the number of people who would see me racing with a branded jersey and the impressions that the social media promotion would get, and I related that to recruiting efforts. I didn't get paid to compete doing what I love because I am a professional athlete. I just found the angle that would make someone else pay for me to compete.

One of the ways in which we earned supplement sales for my company LuaVíve was to get the product to our target market, which happened to be CrossFit athletes at the time. We also found that because people didn't recognize our product, they would always choose a bigger name brand over us. This meant we had to figure out a way to get them to try it. Once they tasted our product and got the explanation about it, our in-person sales were much higher than many of the comparable companies. This allowed us to frame our problem correctly.

The best way to get in front of our market was to go to the local CrossFit competitions in Southern California. Over time, we developed a relationship with the biggest competition promoters and figured out what they needed, which happened to be film. We were able to come to an agreement that we would set up a booth for free at the competitions if we could produce a thirty-second-to-one-minute highlight film for them to promote their other competitions. We got a free film guy by making a deal that we would do a profit-share based on any sales directly related to the commercial he made us. The net result was that we didn't pay up front for anything but were able to lock down an event deal and a film partnership. We found the angle. You can, too, because, if you can step back far enough to see a situation to frame it correctly, the angle will become evident.

It is also worth noting that just like the situation above, you should always look for the win-win. Someone doesn't have to lose for you to get what you want, because we aren't playing a zero-sum game.

Generally speaking, you will be able to get what you want by helping others get what they want.

There will always be room for a service-based economy, so don't believe that doing something you love is only possible by having enough money. Money is just the short, obvious answer. You can find your way around that by being creative. The advent of social media and technology means you and I have significantly fewer excuses for avoiding going after our goals.

Thinking we are not creative is also not a good excuse to throw in the towel on things we want to do. Creativity works much like a muscle. If you don't exercise it, it won't be there when you need it. Furthermore, by approaching your problem in the right way, you can begin to figure out the best solution.

First, always begin with the end in mind. Take out a piece of paper and write down a goal that seems difficult to achieve based on capital or resource restrictions, which is where I have found the most success with this strategy. Next, begin making a list with every single way it might be achieved, both possible and impossible. It is important to note that this list isn't meant to only include your great ideas. This list is about flushing out every single possible idea and figuring out where those ideas are leading you.

The only rule is that nothing is too crazy for the list. In fact, it should be so crazy that you would be embarrassed reading it out loud. Spend some time musing over the list and thinking about what each possibility would look like. Take a few days to make the list so you can be sure it is complete. Each of these things will represent a seed for something better to grow. Hopefully, that thing is a creative way to link where you are to where you want to be. I do this with everything from marketing to product launches to getting and aligning major players and assets for company events. During the creative process, nothing is too outlandish to grease the skids.

The key lies in the simplicity of the whole exercise. Just be willing to write down everything you can possibly think of, and within a short amount of time, roads will start appearing to bridge the gap. We have to get better at not restraining our minds and this is one way to practice. The reason people typically believe that the traditional way to get something done is the only way is because alternative ways are never obvious. You must be willing to search deeply, think unconventionally, and go where others won't. Racking your brain for ideas can get frustrating after a while, but that's the trade-off. If you want to survive when you're small, you have to be scrappy. If you want to thrive, you have to be creative.

Applause waits on success

"Don't go around saying the world owes you a living. The world owes you nothing. It was here first."
−Mark Twain

There was never a shortage of people who doubted I would make it through a special warfare selection program. I like to believe that this is more of a testament to the high attrition rate than to my perceived ability, but either way, those were the cards I was dealt. I fought hard to overcome those cards and make it through on my first attempt. That accomplishment felt good and carried me far in life, giving me direction and opportunities I would never have come across in any other way.

We can be quick to mistake past success for guaranteed future success when they really aren't related. Fast forward ten years, and I am transitioning out of the military into civilian life. If I am not careful, believing that results will come to me in whatever I try next might be easy because I succeeded in the past. I write a lot about entitlement and the crippling role it plays in attempts at success, and this is a subtle way that I have seen it creep into my own life. Believing you are owed something simply because you want it will never be enough to grasp it.

Success worthy of the effort required takes a lot of time. That can be frustrating when you live in a society that is long on expectations and short on patience. Even so, that doesn't change the fact that we need to be willing to slog it out for long periods of time if we want to prevail.

The military makes up one percent of the population. Special forces make up one percent of the military. I was a student and instructor in a special warfare selection course with one of the highest attrition rates of any course in the world, where we were looking for that one percent. Why do people quit this course? The truth is, it's almost never one thing. Typically, every student will find something difficult for them. Between the water, the land, the obstacle courses, and the classroom, there is something that gets extremely tough for everyone. Typically, though, that one thing isn't enough to actually make someone quit. It just happens to suck a little more than the others.

Instead, it's everything together that usually makes people quit. The grind breaks people. Getting up before the sun with sore muscles, feeling your chafing scabs break and tear from between your legs as you jog toward breakfast, staring at the black, cold water at four o'clock in the morning on a swim day, and knowing what lies ahead of you are what break people. People simply break from the monotony of the grind. In my experience, more people quit in the morning on the way to breakfast than any other single time. Many people want to call home and tell their family and friends that they are special forces, but when push comes to shove, the idea of that feeling is not enough to outlast the brutality of the grind.

We must remember that past work isn't always indicative of present success. Can there be crossover? Of course, but you aren't going to break through the noise without doing your time. Be willing to work and run into the wind longer than other people, and you will enjoy more success than them. Be willing to stare cold, black water in the face and dive in day after day. Be willing to endure long enough, and eventually you become the one percent of the one percent.

Chapter 6. Motion

"No man has the right to be an amateur in the matter of physical training. It is a shame for a man to grow old without seeing the beauty and strength of which his body is capable."
—Socrates

It is the absence of motion that is to blame for an overwhelming majority of the issues facing the human animal in this century. The absence of motion toward the things we really want creates resentment. The absence of motion simply for the sake of it creates a frame incapable of going after what we really want. It is a sedentary state that creates the conditions for a denigrated mindset. We are creatures who find their roots in the nomadic tribes of the ancient world and who suffered long hours on foot to survive. Our spirit is stifled when we forget that. If we want to thrive, we should know that physical movement, regardless of its expression, should always be our constant in a sea of variables.

The life cycle of potential

Decay is the inevitable state of everything in the physical world. The only way to even remotely slow that process is to push back against gravity with both motion and resistance. This means that movement is one of the few ways to truly widen your window of potential. Since so much of our time is spent between gestation and development, and then more between atrophy and death, our actual time to express who we are and do the things that we want to in this life is actually quite limited, let's say between eighteen and seventy-six years of age. At eighteen, you're mostly fumbling through life and don't really know what you want or what you are doing, so you spend much of your time trying to compare yourself to other people's potential rather than manifesting your own. This continues for a few years—ten if you're me.

Then we have to factor in cognitive and physical decline. Testosterone and other important hormones begin decreasing rapidly in your fifties, so let's give a liberal estimation and say that your peak opportunity to grow starts to decrease around age sixty. Now, let's finally factor in sleep. The average person spends roughly twenty-six years of their life sleeping. So, you see, the lifecycle of our potential is actually quite short, and that's only if we are one of the lucky ones who live long enough to reach the average. We must come to terms with this short window so we can lean into the time we have..

The human frame is creaky, the fabric is easily torn, and the engine runs rough after a while. What's more, parts are extremely expensive to replace, and as far as maintenance plans go, fixing health problems after they arise is an inefficient way to go about business. Your body is your only vehicle, and although it may be temperamental at times, it is the only means you have to see and do all the things that belong in your stories and not on your bucket list, in your memories and not in your hopes.

Our bodies, like a diesel engine, need to be run often if they are going to operate at capacity. Truthfully, since we are talking maintenance, the best thing you can do for your health is simply take an interest in it. Figure out what your body responds well to and what it responds poorly to. Read books, learn from others who have already walked the path, and don't be afraid to experiment. Once you begin to play with the potential of what your body is capable of, witnessing the unfolding of your evolutionarily engineered biology operating at its peak is one of life's greatest pleasures.

I advocate for setting your couch on fire in large part because the couch is the perfect metaphor for all things sedentary in Western culture. I hope motion takes its place. While your nightly six-pack of beer is spoon-feeding you intellectually lazy information via SportsCenter and CNN, and while you are busy growing out, not up, the best things in life are waiting for you.

Nothing replaces the basics

Experts and gurus often complicate a topic. This is especially true in the fitness world. To remain relevant as they guard the gate of information, I suppose, they talk above the heads of laypeople. Because the principles of kinesiology and bioenergetics come with hard-to-pronounce terms and complicated theories, it is easy for people to take advantage of a consumer who feels lost in it all. For this reason, many of the knowledgeable business owners in the space have no quantifiable reason to help you out of the dark.

And though the body is certainly complicated and health can be a struggle to manage, that does not mean it's impossible. That does not mean the basic tenets of health aren't manageable. The information is pretty much all open source, and it only requires a bit of work on our end. We must be willing to put in the work intellectually and manage the stress physically every day because the truth is we have to be willing to suffer a bit for the results we want. As stated previously, it is our distinct pleasure to suffer in a direction that gives us a say in the way we evolve. For millions of years, creatures didn't even have the capacity to imagine such a thing, let alone act on it.

Three main tenets must be kept up to preserve or improve your physical health. When one of these tenets isn't maintained properly or paid enough attention to, the other two will pick up the slack for a while. After a time, the imbalance will begin to manifest in other places as things begin trying to do work they weren't meant to do. Neglecting one tenet for too long will lead to injuries, both physically and mentally, not to mention chronic underperformance. When we talk about health, what we mean is harmony. Each part of your system works together with the others in order to create an environment that maintains life.

It's no secret that many of the principles covered in this book have stemmed from making physical fitness a priority. I can attribute almost everything worthwhile that I have ever accomplished in life to the upkeep of my physical presence. Even things that I have achieved scholastically wouldn't have been possible without leveraging fitness and making it work for me versus fighting it or simply trying to maintain health with modern medicine. Your overall health is made up of your **diet**, your **movement**, and your **sleep**. When those three tenets meet a strong mental game, you become unstoppable. Only, it's even better than that because, when these three are in alignment, you *do* have a strong mental game. It all feeds off itself, and nothing can be separated from the whole that is you.

When I was struggling to get my supplement company off the ground, I started working a lot. I would be up until midnight or two in the morning every night, and then I would drag myself out of bed for my day job at six or seven in the morning. On at least three days per week, I would get up at four in the morning to push the product to morning gym users. Almost every weekend, we either had an event to work or I used my time to catch up on things I had missed throughout the week, like emails and sales calls.

Fitness was my whole life. Ironically, at the same time that I was operating a fitness business, I was swiftly driving my health into the ground. I justified my declining health because, as mentioned earlier, I felt as though sacrifice was necessary. What I did not understand is that the thing you are not expected to sacrifice is yourself. If the journey is not at least as good as the destination, it's a bad deal. When you have your health and feel good, even the difficult things can provide enjoyment. When you don't have your health, we suffer through even the joyous things in life.

I have talked to gym owners everywhere who have experienced the same thing. The early stages of a business can require brutal hours. Countless gym owners start one because they love the fitness lifestyle and then end up resenting it because they are in the gym all day, every day and never actually work out. What I didn't realize at the time was that by giving a small portion of my time to fitness, I could exponentially multiply my work efficiency and capability.

Figure out a way to keep your health a priority, or it will make itself one. As my health declined and my stress climbed, I noticed that many parts of my life were becoming worse. I became irritable. I was tired but couldn't sleep. Normal activities that I normally loved, like snowboarding and sex, became a chore. This lasted about eight months before I woke up to the tragedies caused by my shortsighted approach to life.

Every aspect of your life should serve you, not limit you. Falling off the path from time to time is okay. To prioritize things so they serve your immediate needs for a moment is okay, but this can easily spiral out of control. We were not meant to be sedentary beings, and if you force yourself to become one, your performance will suffer in all areas of life. You will cease to be the kind of creature you evolved to be. What you actually become is not pretty.

First things first, get your mind right

Writing this book dominated my life, not unlike a new business. I had to spend every hour I was not at work or running my business laboring over the keyboard. As it was a side hustle, I needed to use my time as effectively as possible. To do that, I needed to ensure that I was firing on all cylinders so I could try to induce a flow state as quickly as possible. If the work you do requires mental capacity in any form, it can be helpful to figure out a way to leverage the timeline of your day so you can be as effective as possible. Thirty minutes of morning cardio at roughly sixty percent effort can get your mind going for hours. Lunchtime walks can keep it going. There are countless ways to leverage your time, and they don't all require you to suffer.

When you are engaged in any kind of work, flow state is arguably the most important thing you can harness. The ultimate goal when you are working on anything that requires cognitive ability is to get into flow. This is what people describe as "getting in the zone." Almost all of us know what that feeling is like. The ideas come to you with little effort, you see things before they happen, and your brain is seemingly working on a level above what it does on your day-to-day tasks. It's a beautiful thing when it happens, because you are able to get some of your best work done with relative ease. It's what allows you to focus without distraction on a cognitively demanding task.

While stimulants, such as caffeine or methamphetamine (the main ingredient found in Adderall), may help induce a state of flow while you're working, using stimulants is a flawed plan for continued success. The problem with most stimulants is that they are borrowed energy, meaning you will have to pay it back. The more artificial energy you borrow from caffeine, sugar, and carbohydrates, the more you will pay back in the form of energy crashes later in the day. Sugar, for example, causes your blood glucose levels to spike, and nothing in this life goes up without coming down.

Continuing this throughout the day puts your brain on a roller coaster and makes getting off that roller coaster especially challenging when you are ready to. Such is the case when you want to go to bed at night. The sleep cycle known as your circadian rhythm gets interrupted from all of the peaks and valleys, and you end up in a constant game of catch-up, over-caffeinating when you need energy, and unable to sleep when it's time to pay that energy back. This is not a sustainable way to live your life. Your roller coaster will eventually run out of tracks.

When you enhance your cognitive function through movement, such as exercise, you are not borrowing nearly as much. The energy lasts longer and is much slower to leave you. Exercise increases memory, enhances focus, and dramatically improves mood. I have personally found the changes it brings about to be far more beneficial than what you get from drinking a Red Bull. The sweet spot is when you leverage exercise to get your mind running and then add in a little frothy caffeinated goodness to improve the state rather than achieve the state.

John J. Ratey is an MD and associate clinical professor of psychiatry at Harvard Medical School. He has made it his life's work to explore the connection between exercise and brain function. In his book *Spark*, he walks through the research that helps us understand the brain-body connection. The following is the introduction to *Spark*, which summarizes the point well without getting you lost in technical speak and medical jargon.

> We all know that exercise makes us feel better, but most of us have no idea why. We assume it's because we're burning off stress or reducing muscle tension or boosting endorphins, and we leave it at that. But the real reason we feel so good when we get our blood pumping is that it makes the brain function at its best, and in my

view, this benefit of physical activity is far more important—and fascinating—than what it does for the body. Building muscles and conditioning the heart and lungs are essentially side effects. I often tell my patients that the point of exercise is to build and condition the brain.

In today's technology-driven, plasma-screened-in world, it's easy to forget that we are born movers—animals, in fact—because we've engineered movement right out of our lives. Ironically, the human capacity to dream and plan and create the very society that shields us from our biological imperative to move is rooted in the areas of the brain that govern movement. As we adapted to an ever-changing environment over the past half million years, our thinking brain evolved from the need to hone motor skills. We envision our hunter-gatherer ancestors as brutes who relied primarily on physical prowess, but to survive over the long haul they had to use their smarts to find and store food. The relationship between food, physical activity, and learning is hardwired into the brain's circuitry.

But we no longer hunt and gather, and that's a problem. The sedentary character of modern life is a disruption of our nature, and it poses one of the biggest threats to our continued survival. Evidence of this is everywhere: 65 percent of our nation's adults are overweight or obese, and 10 percent of the population has type 2 diabetes, a preventable and ruinous disease that stems from inactivity and poor nutrition. Once an affliction almost exclusively of the middle-aged, it's now becoming an epidemic among children. We're literally killing ourselves, and it's a problem throughout the developed world, not merely a province of the supersize lifestyle in the United States. What's even more disturbing, and what virtually no one recognizes, is that inactivity is killing our brains too—physically shriveling them.

Cycle stress

Most health and fitness trainers understand that the body gets stronger and fitter through a linear progression that is contingent on leveraging the principle of overload. The principle of overload states:

> A greater than normal stress or load on the body is required for training adaptation to take place. The body will adapt to this stimulus. Once the body has adapted then a different stimulus is required to continue the change. For a muscle to increase strength, it must be gradually stressed by working against a load greater than it is used to.

That gradual stress is known as a linear progression.

The part that is missing from the principle of overload is the idea of a deload period. Typically, the volume of a program is increased over a few weeks, say three, and then the volume is taken away for a week, and something like active recovery, which includes mobilizing or yoga, light cardio movement, or even much lighter weight training, takes its place. Rest periods allow the body time to recover and adapt to the new stressors it has been put under.

In short, this means that adding more and more volume does not equal more and more success. You can't just continue to stack more and more stress, thinking it will continue to yield results at the same rate at which you are adding stress. In reality, it would look more like stress + stress + stress + rest = success. The only time you actually get stronger is during the rest period.

This is the basic underlying idea behind every good strength and conditioning plan that has ever been written. Stress the muscles under more and more tension in a progressive manner, allow the body time to recover, adjust, and grow to meet the demands of this new stress, and then restart the process. It also happens to be the basic underlying idea behind every facet of life in which you might want to succeed, whether health, creativity, business, or intellectual thought. This is the cycle that makes muscle growth possible, because that's where we've learned to apply it. In reality, this is the process that makes all human growth possible. You cannot remain buried in your work forever, thinking that the results will be exponential and equal to the amount of work you put in. Many entrepreneurs would be disappointed to realize that their success would be increased if they took the dreaded off-day.

The concept of progressive overload only stimulates a response when the body has time to respond. You can hustle and work hard for a while, but eventually you need to process the work you have done. Our bodies and minds need time to adjust and grow from the new stimulus that has been put on them. Taking time to heal and grow is fundamental to human biology.

Chapter 7. The Bucket List Blueprint

"So we shall let the reader answer this question for himself: who is the happier man, he who has braved the storm of life and lived or he who has stayed securely on shore and merely existed?"
– Hunter S. Thompson

There is no replacement for experience when it comes to understanding yourself and figuring out where you fit into the unfolding of creation. Unfortunately, it is all too easy to find yourself with a long list of "one days" and "hopefullys," as in, "One day, I'd love to go skydiving or see the Grand Canyon, and hopefully, I can make enough money now so that later I can do what I want." As we progress in life, we find that all of these hopes are comfortable on a bucket list or in a conversation over cocktails. As more time passes, something interesting happens, which is that, psychologically speaking, these things get further away from our capability. It's like anything difficult in life. The longer you ignore it, the bigger it gets, and the smaller you get. Eventually it will become an "I should have," and a life with too many of those starts to get painful. Oftentimes, when we can't escape the pain of not being the person we know we could be, so we spend our time escaping from our lives.

Exploration and its accompanying curiosity are often ignited when you begin exposing yourself to new experiences, regardless of what they are. Over time, some of those experiences resonate with some part of you, sparking a desire for further investigation. This curiosity can also be ignited when you are exposed to a person who has experienced so much of life that their curiosity and passion are contagious.

As we've discussed, what you are exposed to throughout your lifetime is what you will know as reality, and that will dictate what you believe is possible. Further, what you've experienced will inform the world you currently look at. If you spend a majority of your life around the same people in the same place, those people and that place inform your mental setpoint or homeostasis. Just like the "hopefullys" you never contend with on your bucket list, other people, places, and cultures that you avoid tend to feel threatening over time. The outer limits of what is possible will always be governed by the reality that you do not take the time to question.

Just like the success we spoke of earlier, difficult things in life can be broken down into easily manageable parts. The bucket list blueprint is a way of doing that. Over time, your engagement with life will teach you to stretch yourself when needed and complete things that you never thought possible. Impossible, then, is a process. Rather than waiting on your ship to come in, you can take a systematic approach to building it. Whether what you hope to achieve is physical or intellectual is irrelevant because the approach is the same. The deconstruction of the task is the same. The effort is the same. Most importantly, the idea of breaking complex experiences down to their most basic elements is the same.

This blueprint is a reflection of that effort and deconstruction. It is a replication of the exact approach I have taken to running ultra-marathons with very little preparation time, to founding a company with absolutely no experience, and to finishing at the top of my class in one of the most academically rigorous special forces schools in the United States military despite the fact that I was technically not qualified to be there because of my aptitude examination. On the surface, these things seemingly have nothing in common with each other, but the fact is that each of them seemed well beyond the realm of possibility for me to figure out and accomplish.

This blueprint is how I ran that first fifty-mile race that I mentioned at the beginning of the prologue. At five foot ten' and 230 pounds, I did not have what most would consider a runner's body, to say the least. As mentioned before, I had not even run over three miles in the past year. I felt much more comfortable with weights in the gym than trails in the mountains.

Seven weeks before I took the starting line for my first fifty-mile race, I couldn't run more than a mile and a half without stopping and stretching my cramped calves. I went out on a two-mile run and found myself doubled over on the sidewalk and infuriated with my lack of cardiovascular conditioning. Desperately wishing to be torn from my comfort zone and somewhat angry about my own lack of ability, I found the most brutal run I could and signed up for it. An ultra-marathon had sat on my bucket list for years, comfortably lying in my future. With a strong desire to conquer inability, I took the starting line less than two months later at five in the morning and ran over four times longer than I had ever run in my life. Over fifteen times longer than my current conditioning at the time I signed up. This process will help you understand how.

I also struggled in school. I dropped out of college the second I realized I didn't have to be there. School was always a struggle because I was generally disinterested in the curriculum. I viewed the military as my only option of escaping my hometown and seeing the world while simultaneously circumnavigating college. When I arrived at the special operations combat medic course, I sat in a class consisting of almost all college graduates and doctors. A bit intimidated, I knew at that moment I would have to overcome years of skipping class and working lackadaisically at projects. I would have to do what my teachers had been on my back for me to do my entire life and "apply myself."

I don't say any of this to brag, because I know there is nothing inherently special about me. I have no hidden talents—in fact, probably the opposite: it usually feels like I am trekking uphill most of the time. The difference is that I figured out a system that allows me to take something intimidating and make it manageable. That is what you must always know about daring to do great and seemingly impossible things; there is always a way to systematize the process of achieving them.

Everything that we do, we do because we have figured out systems and developed tools that allow us to do those things. Humans are not especially set up to dominate the food chain. In fact, for a large part of our existence, we resided somewhere in the middle, hunting, gathering, and hoping something bigger or stronger did not develop a taste for our flesh. Two thumbs and a developed prefrontal cortex gave us the ability to create machinery to separate us from the wild we climbed out of. We're not especially set up to fly, either, but you can be on the other side of the world in a day and a half if you really want to be. What makes humanity great is our ability to create systems to do things that previously lay outside of our grasp.

The best part is that when you leverage this system, life becomes much more exciting. You don't have to sit around dreaming about what your life could be, only to wake to the nightmare that you're actually living. You simply figure out what you want it to be (or what you think you want it to be) and then start taking steps to get there. Rather than waiting on the capability to one day arrive, you can stick to pragmatic steps that let you take stock of your progress, desire, and capability.

The bucket list has become the most underused tool we have in our arsenal for creating a life we want. A bucket list is essentially a list of experiences or achievements a person hopes to have or accomplish during their lifetime. Sometimes the list is kept on a sheet of paper, but more often than not, it consists of semi-formed ideas about things we could do that rattle around in our mind whenever something reminds us of it. Typically, a bucket list also consists of the things that you think are awesome but subconsciously believe you could never really do.

This is one reason why, after their first skydiving jump, people land on the ground with a massive smile from ear to ear. Yes, dopamine, and yes, they are happy to be alive and back on the ground in one piece. But this also gives a person the feeling that they have just transcended what is possible. The smile sits on the intersection of pride, disbelief, and awe. A small subset of the population experiences this feeling all the time. They are the high performers who make us all sit wide-eyed on the sidelines, questioning what we previously thought possible.

There is also a part of your soul that comes alive as you begin to see your own capabilities grow in comparison to your older perceived limitations. This might be where you hear the term "self-transcendence." You transcend the limits of your old self, and in doing so, you embody more of your true strength and power.

People who don't engage with their lives in this way tend to become the person on the sidelines who condemns someone every time they take a risk in life or consider doing so. They tell people they aren't capable of things that they want to do because they are projecting all the things that they couldn't or didn't do onto others. They become crabs in a bucket.

When a fisherman catches a crab, he throws it in a white five-gallon bucket with the rest of the crabs. He knows he doesn't need to put a cover on the bucket. If you sit there and watch them, you'll see some of the crabs trying desperately to climb to the top of the bucket and escape. The other crabs, though, will never allow that. In their own desperate, uncalculated attempts to save their lives, they will continue to reach up and pull the other crabs that have a shot down, ensuring that everyone becomes food together. Learn from the crabs. Some will feel inclined to pull you down because they are panicked and don't know what else to do. Others may even want you at the bottom simply because misery does love company. In any case, you are not obligated to drown with anyone.

So, now it's time to resurrect your bucket list and figure out what items you have been longing to do. If you don't have one, take about thirty minutes and sit down with this one. Just like when coming up with creative angles, let your mind really expand and just put things down on paper. This step is crucial because it is often our own judgments about what our lives should look like that keep our minds from going where they really want. Even if you arrive only to find that you are not completely in love with all the fantasies you thought you would be, which is bound to happen, at least you will know that and have a much better idea about what you really want your life to look like. Without garnering experiences, your life becomes a reflection of what you could have done but didn't do. It's painful to see and even more painful to live.

Life has layers. The beauty you see in each layer is equal to the degree in which you experience it. As an example, consider a sunrise. A beautifully taken photo by a talented photographer using quality equipment can render a beautiful picture that inspires something like awe and admiration. This is level one. If you happen to be driving and can pull over to a bluff and see that same sunrise in person, you realize that no picture will do its magnificence justice. You are experiencing the second layer of what life has to offer. If you climb a mountain or hike to that same bluff with a loved one, only to arrive sweaty and determined, having worked hard to earn the view of a rising sun with your own two feet, you'll feel a connectedness to that beauty that is not possible any other way. You have penetrated into life's depth. You simply won't know if you want to climb mountains by looking at pictures your whole life. You can try to articulate what life is about, but its meaning is really only revealed in the depth of experience.

I was on day three of a two-hundred-five-mile race through the mountains when I happened to reach a peak at sunset. Coming off an intense climb, I sat for a moment at the summit with my pacer, whom I had somehow convinced to accompany me on this particularly rough leg of the race. We were enjoying a brownie I had packed and appreciating the brilliant colors streaming across the sky. Anyone who has tried to recreate that moment by taking a photo to show others knows it is impossible. The best that you can do is just be. Just appreciate the moment for what it is. I had reached what is perhaps the deepest feeling of life that exists in the physical world. I had suffered for something beautiful. Endless ways to recreate this feeling in life exist, from the birth of a child to the creation of a realized project. Generally, the more pain you suffer, the more beauty you experience, and the deeper you get to feel as a reward.

Every single time you cross something off your bucket list, you go a layer deeper into experience and life. You know more, and you're closer to finding the life you want, separating what you love from what you love the idea of. As a quick disclaimer and as someone who has spent a great deal of time chasing after mountaintops of various sizes, a little perspective comes in handy. Realize that the point of life isn't about arriving at a single destination; instead, it is about the inner evolution that takes place from searching for many different destinations and immersing yourself in as many layers of life as possible.

The bucket list blueprint is meant to help you begin doing that. It is important to note that this blueprint won't deliver all your dreams on a silver platter. It is more of a road map to enable you to look for them yourself. In other words, the blueprint doesn't give you the fish; it helps you figure out if you like fishing before you spend your life buying new reels and staring at a bobber while your actual interests are somewhere on the other side of the world.

The art of the low-risk probe

Like most eighth-graders, I had my heart set on the life of a rock star. I went to one Godsmack concert in eighth grade, and my fate was sealed. A new guitar for Christmas, endless hours in my room smashing away on the thing, and I knew it was only a matter of time.

Fast forward ten years, and I'm playing in a local band in Virginia Beach called Midnight Lineup, a name we picked after a surf town in southern Brazil. We made the band up in a quick-witted scheme to get girls in a bar in Rio de Janeiro. Eventually we actually had to play music, as the bar had their band cancel. Two people who had never played with each other figured out a way to fumble through a few Sublime cover songs.

When we got back, we started playing more music together because it had been so fun. I mentioned that I liked to write songs, and soon we were playing almost all originals and building a small group of friends who liked to come to shows and parties and yell our lyrics. Eventually we got a song on the local radio station and started wondering if we should try and do this more seriously.

We played a few local shows, which was an experience that would have made eighth-grade-me proud as hell. I got to feel what it was like when the crowd in a dark room yells, "Encore! Encore! Encore!" and hopes you'll come play just a few more songs. This is something I will have forever.

I realized in the end that the grind of playing music wasn't going to be for me. I grew to hate the late nights in the studio and almost everything that comes with the life that my small taste of the music industry involved. But I know that now because I got to live through it. I saw a childhood dream through, and what did it cost me? A few epic years of playing music and partying with my friends. I'll take it.

During one of our final shows, I caught my reflection in the mirror right before I went on stage. I remember seeing myself and hearing the crowd. I remember knowing that I wouldn't do this forever but I was doing it now and that was all that mattered. I was soaking it up, and I loved every second of it. This was my first understanding of the low-risk probe. What few people realize, either because they have lied to themselves or others have lied to them, is that everyone can live their dreams in some capacity.

The low-risk probe (LRP) is a concept that allows you to test the waters without the risk of drowning. After gathering all the information possible, which could just be a Google search, depending on the complexity of what you want to achieve, a low-risk probe is the concept of figuring out the minimum barrier to entry with the minimum investment of both time and money. This step is key to moving onto new horizons while still being able to exit should you find yourself unhappy or unwilling to continue moving forward with your pursuit. If being a rock star is the dream, Midnight Lineup is the LRP. If running a marathon is the goal, a weekend five-kilometer race is the LRP. If going into business for yourself is the goal, starting a side hustle while continuing to work your job is the LRP.

One thing to note is that the LRP isn't necessarily easier than going all in. It is just about managing the downside and risk *before* you go all in. In the case of the side business, for example, it isn't going to be easy. You will need to really put in a lot of hours outside of work, not just in your business but *on* your business. The learning curve will be steep, but if you get into the business and realize you don't like the industry or the pressure of owning and operating, or you find a host of other reasons that businesses fail, in the end, you haven't given up anything. The monetary loss should be minimized, and the knowledge gained should be maximized. Those two things are always the main goals of the low-risk probe. You still have your job, and you will have learned a ton, which can only make you better in other areas of your life. Just like everything in life, don't think easy; think worth it. Think, manage risk, learn what you need to, and allow yourself to test the waters.

The milestone approach

With each endeavor that you set, the LRP provides a safe barrier. You just need to make sure it doesn't stay that way—unless, of course, you are unhappy, in which case, the experiment is over, and your life is a little bit closer to where you want it to be. Coming up with milestones along the way is critically important to know whether you are moving forward or not.

Let's look at the business idea. At what point do you know you are ready to quit your job? Do you need to replace a certain amount of income? These are the things that you need to figure out. The more detailed each milestone is, the better off you will be. By starting with the end in mind (the overall dream) and then figuring out your starting point (the LRP), you then begin dividing the in-between work up into manageable parts. You don't have to know necessarily everything in between because you'll learn as you go; you just have to start figuring it out. The milestones aren't things you must do. They just give you a way to check the temperature while the heat rises. They give you a guide that helps you see if you are making progress.

In the information age, everything is open source. With millions of people consistently producing free content via electronic-format books, YouTube videos, podcasts, and whatever other media arise, nothing is off limits or unattainable when it comes to knowledge about any given endeavor. Of course, this means you must vet your source and information and know that what you are consuming is quality, but consumer responsibility aspects of the technological age aside, humans have never been more uniquely positioned to do anything they desire in life. I literally just finished a business class at Stanford University via iTunes U, free of charge, while on the treadmill every morning. Despite never applying to Stanford or even leaving my house, I was able to gain world-class education to help me build my business and create wealth. That is the power of where we are in the timeline of existence.

Having such abundant knowledge at our fingertips has positioned us to get wherever we want in life. I suggest using that information to formulate the milestone approach. Figure out what the milestones are that you will need to achieve to get where you want after formulating your LRP. These will act as an outline to guide you through training or preparation for what you want. If you want to physically go somewhere you have never been, then you need to follow a map; these milestones will help you build your own map to get you where you are trying to go, whether that's the finish line of a marathon or publishing a book.

The very first thing you need to do is start with the end in mind. What, specifically, does success look like for what you are trying to do? This is the item from your bucket list you are pursuing. From there, no matter how lofty the goals, you need to break that down into smaller, manageable goals that will eventually get you closer to what you want. As you will see, this can be done in really creative ways.

The most important first phase of the milestone approach is that you pick a measurable and tangible goal, something to which metrics can be applied to determine whether you are progressing or not. Differentiate between a goal and a wish and then go with the goal.

As long as I've been alive, simply wishing something would happen has never willed it to be. Once the penny leaves your hand for the fountain, it's gone. End of story. Your wish is no more likely to come true than you are to find your penny at the water's bottom with all the other dreams that have been left for dead. Even Merriam-Webster recognizes the chances of your wish coming true as poor; "wish" is defined as "to want something that cannot or probably will not come true." Dreams, then, must be rooted in something you can measure and attain.

The last note about goal-setting is that for best success with the milestones, shoot for goals that can be achieved in a short amount of time. At first, easily accessible goals are advisable. Learn from everyone who buys a gym membership in January and doesn't see a weight again all year long. To start, keep it less than ninety days. It is extremely hard to stick with something, especially something new, for a prolonged period. You want motivation to stay high as you work hard in new territory. Even if, realistically, your main goal could take six-months to six years, breaking the first goal down to ninety days and never going ninety days without another milestone is a recommended way to ensure you stay on track.

The second step is to research every possible nuance concerning whatever you want to accomplish. Figure out what the research and experts recommend as far as training and structure and then account for your physical limitations, time constraints, and knowledge. This is where knowing how to find a creative angle can be helpful.

When I wanted to run fifty-four miles in an ultra-marathon only a few months away, despite having very little running experience, my thought process went something like this. My ultimate goal was to run fifty-four miles, which was my measurable end state. I knew I needed to get my body used to working for long hours at a time, as the race would take about twelve hours if all went well. I knew my body would never be able to handle that kind of running volume in its present state, as I had not built up my joints to handle the pounding. I also knew I had been lifting weights heavily for the past year and, if I worked it right, I could use that to my advantage. Conventional wisdom said I needed my longest-mileage day to be twenty-five to thirty miles before the race. This was my longest non-negotiable milestone. I worked backward and made two more milestones that would allow me to get to that bigger one. My first long milestone was eleven miles, and the second was eighteen miles. Lastly, I knew I wouldn't even be able to handle running the milestone without risking injuries associated with overuse, such as stress fractures and plantar fasciitis, so they would have to be attained in some other way.

    With a quick Google search, I found that experts say the run-to-bike ratio is roughly one to three, meaning one mile of running is equal to three miles of biking as far as exertion goes. The last obstacle I had to overcome was the fact that the course I had signed up for, in North Carolina, had hills amounting to about eight thousand feet of elevation gain and loss, and where I lived in Virginia Beach did not. Due to my work schedule, getting anywhere with hills to train proved to be extremely difficult. This was where my gym background helped. Box step-ups and lunges sandwiched between cardio helped mimic the effects of the hills on my legs.

Although running fifty-four miles after never going longer than a half-marathon seemed like a stretch, to say the least, I knew I could use rational, sound logic to think my way through the problem, provided my actions followed suit. While some factors may not have measured up exactly how I hoped, the logic held up enough to get me through the race. I was never in danger of winning, or even coming close to the podium. I also did not fail to meet my goal. All things considered, I was able to break down a lifetime goal into manageable steps, accomplish it within a short period of time, use that experience as the introduction to this book, and fall in love with a whole new sport in the process. That is the power of the bucket list blueprint. It seems like small things that may be inconsequential, but this life will always reveal more of itself if you have the courage to take the path.

Don't be afraid to quit

The bravado of Western culture has done well at labeling quitting as failing and treating it like it is a sin against God. As with much of this book, however, a certain reframing of thought processes is in order. The inherent problem with always framing quitting as failing is that it insinuates you should always press on regardless of the circumstances. This logic might hold up if time were an unlimited resource, but you and I know that isn't the case. Carrying on with something you don't enjoy and is meaningless to you is a wasteful way to spend your time. Under the right circumstances, quitting isn't just acceptable; it is advisable

The reverse side of this coin is that quitting should never be your first option. People who are heavy on ambition and light on follow-through have very little to show for all of their great ideas. It can be helpful to establish "quit" or "don't quit" parameters for a situation. Being aware of when you should or shouldn't quit something before heading into any given endeavor will help you make the decision with clarity. When the pressure, stress, or pain sets in, you won't be subject to the whims of negative thought or momentary weakness. Instead, you can make your decision knowing full well the consequences of your choice.

When I was going through the special forces selection process, not quitting was the absolute most important thing besides performing. In that scenario, quitting meant failure, not doing what I signed up to do, and spending the rest of my military enlistment in a job I didn't want. I knew what quitting meant, and I was aware of what would happen should I choose to no longer continue training.

Although it was difficult, even miserable at times, those were necessary evils to get where I wanted in life and to accomplish what I wanted. In this case, before beginning the selection course, I knew that I was going into a "no fail" scenario where I would not quit no matter the pain. For some things in life, this is the decision. What you are weighing is whether the outcome is worth any amount of discomfort in the world. In this situation, it was. Possibly what you want to do is the same way. It is also entirely impossible that what you want to achieve might be attained through some other method. In the selection course, there was no other way to get to the end state, so the decision of whether to quit or not was a no-brainer. In your current or desired situation, that may not be the case. Many people stay in jobs they hate and finish reading books they are uninterested in because they're so conditioned by our success at all cost's mentality.

Compare that exact scenario to the very first business that I started. I knew that I wanted to own my own business, and I knew that I wanted to build it around a lifestyle that I loved. The goal was that I would have total freedom and spend every day making a difference in the community, which happened to be fitness. Not really knowing how to begin, I started with my LRP, printing t-shirts and calling it an "athletic apparel" company. The only problem is that I had no unique ideas or appreciable skills to make the business work. I found myself much more in the textile industry than the athletic world, and every day was a struggle to figure out how to sell anything. After about a year of struggling, I came to the realization that I didn't have the passion to make it work.

My first thought was to tell people that I was closing the business. I didn't want to be a quitter, and I most certainly did not want to be perceived as a failure. One of the many lessons I learned from starting my first business was that other people's opinions of you are not enough reason to spend your time being miserable. In fact, I would take it a step further and say that there is nothing worth being miserable for unless it is a means to an end and those means are justified by your end. Ask yourself if doing this thing gets you where you truly want to be. That is the only reason to do things you hate. No exceptions. Weigh the result of quitting and compare it to what you will be missing. Consider your desired end state and spend time thinking about whether it could be reached by some other means; then act accordingly. Make your plan to quit on a sunny day so you don't end up regretting it if you quit in the middle of a storm.

Burn Your Couch

The result of quitting my athletic apparel endeavor was that I learned a lot about what I didn't want to do. I learned countless lessons about how to start and run a business. I learned the legalities behind business structure and operations. I learned what worked for marketing and what did not. Essentially, I received a year-long crash course on entrepreneurship, and the whole thing cost me about three thousand dollars total when it was all said and done. Armed with so much more knowledge about starting a business, and specifically what I wanted out of running my own business, my second venture met with more success. Once it was time, quitting was the best thing I could have done for myself and my future.

I cannot tell you where your quitting point lies, and you cannot tell anyone else where their quitting point lies. Many businesses and individuals have persisted long after people have written them off, only to succeed later in life. Many people have also persisted after people have written them off and subsequently burned through all their cash and ended up with nothing. To avoid ending up like one of the latter, use the low-risk probe. Ask yourself difficult questions about how you are liking the process. Trust your intuition about whether you see yourself doing your project long term.

Motivation is overrated

> *"Do or do not. There is no try."*
> *—Yoda*

We often mistakenly mislabel the things that are indescribable with the word "impossible." Here's what I mean. An athlete does something extraordinary, leaving fans' jaws dropped and setting a new bar for what humans are capable of (think back to Roger Banister and his four-minute mile). An interviewer immediately rushes over to gush and asks the athlete how they did it and what was going through their mind.

Often there was literally nothing going through their mind because they had entered a state of flow in which the encumbered normal waking consciousness was transcended. Superhuman feats often require that we enter supra-human consciousness. Here is where we misunderstand what we just saw.

These sometimes elusive states have been quite well studied and understood. What we know now is that a number of elements must come together at once for the psychological conditions to be right for one to reach a flow state. They occur when someone is rooted in what they know or understand while simultaneously exploring what they do not know. There must also be a certain amount of risk present to keep one's focus in the now. So, let's talk about how this looks in practice and what it means for our purposes. I'll use two examples, one intellectual and one physical, to highlight this point.

People describe reaching flow states in both surfing and writing. I've loosely entered into one right now as I work on this book. I say "loosely" because, as I write, I am also engaged in self-reflection, and turning the focus back towards oneself can disrupt the flow state. For this reason, performance anxiety is the polar opposite of flow. It's complete focus on self and not on what the self is doing.

If you were to learn how to surf today, reaching a flow state would be extremely difficult because your proficiency would not be high enough to let go of your focus on self. To use previous words, the conditions are not right because you are not rooted in what you know. You must be comfortable enough to let your actions become autonomic and without your conscious control. If you learn how to surf well enough to do it without thinking about the steps, and then you catch a wave, you are physically pushing into the unknown at every moment. The presence of risk is just enough to keep your focus in the present moment, and your proficiency is good enough to keep you from having to over-manage the details. Thus, you will find time slows down (this is a result of your sensory information inputs slicing reality up and giving you more bits of information per second), and because of this, your decision-making capacity is increased. You do not have to labor over what you are doing.

While writing, flow will be hard to reach if you are not confident enough in yourself as a writer to let go and let what is within you emerge. If you are capable of letting yourself simply write, all the same variables apply, and you'll notice that you are psychologically exploring a world you do not yet know. It is not uncommon for writers to write for hours and then read what they wrote and notice that they didn't actually know everything they just wrote down before they wrote it. Writing a fictional story often works in this manner.

Now, let's get back to the athlete who just achieved something inspiring. Typically, the athlete can't really put into words what just happened because, as stated before, they moved beyond their waking consciousness and life lived through them. Often, they'll just talk about how humble and excited they are to have had it all work out.

Something else happens in the minds of onlookers, too. If they find admiration in what they saw, then what they saw is trying to wake something in themselves. Because most of us are programmed to stay comfortable and our own power is extremely uncomfortable to face, we will divorce those qualities from ourselves and project them completely onto the people we are watching. "They could do that, but of course, I never could!" The athletes remain in the realm of impossibility, and we get to safely stay within our limitations.

Not only do these athletes resonate with you because part of your soul is trying to shake off the slumber of the routine, but they are often at the end of an unbroken chain of commitment to practice. The more they are rooted in what they know, the more easily they can access flow. What you are seeing is not a miracle as much as it is a way of living that makes the miraculous possible, even likely.

Many of us sit around, hoping for enough motivation to commit to our lives, and then dismiss what we want as impossible when the reality begins to present itself. Motivation is overrated because there will never be enough of it. You don't need motivation; you need practice. This is not to say that, like Usain Bolt, you can set a world record and win an Olympic medal. I'm saying that if it excites you when you see it, that excitement is some part of your own soul stirring because there is surely something that it does want to do. The adventure of a lifetime is trying to find out what.

Focus on what you can control

As a rule in life, focusing on the things you can control and letting go of what you cannot control is often the better route to inner peace. You must take a step back and figure out the supporting details associated with your venture. These supporting details, the things you can actually control, are the parameters you will act within. The limiting thoughts are often what you must let go of.

As an example, take my first ultra-marathon. I could not control the fact that, with my current body weight and level of deconditioning, I would surely run into overuse injuries if I followed a conventional training plan. Since I still wanted to do the race, this took all conventionality off the table. I spent tons of time with alternative cardio members and accepted that as part of this process. If the plan had a ten mile run, then I had a 30 mile bike ride in my future. Be honest with yourself about your current skill level, what's required, and what you have at your disposal. This will help you create your parameters for action, which will ultimately end up as your milestones.

This blueprint will help you accomplish rather lofty goals quickly if you can find the right angle, and knowing the details is crucial for that. This often means we must let go of what would be nice but isn't currently an option. Pining over what we don't have helps soothe the smallest parts of ourselves, but it can be detrimental to our success.

Keep extending the horizon

There's almost no daylight between the notions of always wanting more because you are fulfilled by the process and never being satisfied because nothing will ever be good enough. It is a thin line that many of the world's highest performers have found themselves on the wrong side of. The only way to win in this scenario is to embrace the process rather than the result. It has taken me a long time to realize this simple fact: Some of the most successful people in the world have become successful by never being truly satisfied with the result.

Some of the happiest people in the world have become happy by falling in love with the journey that yields the results. Both scenarios tend to yield results, but the first one yields an emptiness that isn't worth any achievement.

Steve Jobs pushed for perfection in Apple's innovative products, which resulted in products that were highly successful by every measure. From most accounts I've heard, he was also a miserable person to work for and with. As you look to complete different items on your bucket list, there will undoubtedly be things you don't really care for and others that resonate with you and draw you in. Whether these things are hobbies or something you try to turn into a profession, ensure that you are enjoying the journey before going further. If you are relying on the achievement to fill you up, you should know now that it won't be enough. Often, we like the idea of something (or rather, the idea of having something to put our identity in) so much that we don't stop to realize that chasing it is making us miserable.

That being said, your laurels will become an uncomfortable place to rest after a while. After a longer while, you'll resent them. We must find the balance between evolution and stagnation, and we must also know and give ourselves grace when we mess that balance up. Similar to flow, keep one foot at home and one pushing into the horizon. Evolve with life and find new frontiers that call to you. Backsliding or becoming comfortable in life is okay; that happens. When it does, use your bucket list to break free of that cycle. Once you are moving, the rest is simply a matter of momentum.

Chapter 8. All That's Left Is to Endure

*"Not only so, but also glory in our sufferings, because
we know that suffering produces perseverance;
perseverance, character; and character, hope. And
hope does not disappoint."*
–Romans 5:3–5

Remembering the night that everything collapsed around me is hard to look back on. I was half-yelling in anger and half-whining pathetically, "I want this whole f*cking thing gone," I said and slammed the bottle of Maker's Mark onto the counter. It was my best friend and roommate's bottle, but I had found out that he had died just a moment before. As quickly as I possibly could, I poured myself a shot again and then took it down twice as fast as it took to pour. Without even a breath in between, I did it again. And again. And again. And over and over until I grew so frustrated with the sluggish speed of the consumption method that I eventually tipped the bottom of the bottle to the heavens, a place I was growing to resent, and guzzled what whiskey remained.

Before all went black, I saw a leftover watermelon sitting on the counter, whole and unharmed by the surrounding world. That was a crime I just could not accept. With one motion, I hurled the oblong green fruit and smashed it into a thousand gooey red chunks all over the far side of the kitchen. I was numb at the moment, but I badly wanted to feel. I was broken, and I wanted everything else to be broken, too. I wanted to know what was real and what wasn't, but the systemic Novocain I had been tipping back in the form of Maker's Mark for the past six hours would ensure that I would feel nothing more than a slight tingling, leave all the real pain for the next day.

The next morning, it was the pounding on my front door that brought me back into consciousness. As I awoke, it was the pounding in my head that made me instantly throw up on the floor. Wearily making my way out of bed, stepping over a puddle of my own vomit, and walking down the stairs and to the front door, I was still shaking off the Novocain. Standing in my doorway were four uniformed men, and without any warning, I unequivocally knew exactly what was real. My best friend had given his life in service to his country, and they were at my door to help me go through his belongings before packaging them up and shipping them off to his family in Massachusetts.

The prior day, friends had been over for our weekly barbeque, and at twenty-two years old, these barbecues were much more akin to a high school party than they were casual afternoon get-togethers with adult friends. I had transitioned from the house party to the bar in search of the promised one-dollar Coronas around seven o'clock at night, and I was pretty much blitzed by the time night fell. And that is why, when my friend Jessy came to take me off the dance floor with tears streaming down her face, I couldn't feel anything.

I looked down at my phone and saw thirty-something missed calls. As I did, Jessy cried, "Tyler's gone." At that moment, I realized that life waits for no one to be ready. Some people learn this at a painfully young age, and perhaps I am lucky to have waited so long for the true harshness of reality to penetrate my innocent bubble. In the coming months, I noticed that the world simply spins, emotionless and oblivious to human feelings, circling the sun over and over, regardless of how we live our lives down here or what's going on. I spent the next half of the year doing everything I could to get rid of the feelings I was hoping to experience after that first night.

Drinking day in and day out seemed like the only way my friends and I could cope. Truthfully, when I was drinking was the only time I wasn't absolutely miserable. I have no idea how I kept my job that summer. I almost never went to work, and when I did, I was drunk, wearing someone else's clothes, and completely indifferent to the military's heritage of discipline. I couldn't have cared about the rules, and I wasn't shy about letting people know.

In the beginning of the aftermath, I truly didn't care if I got kicked out of the military, if I stayed in, or if I continued in my purgatory. All that mattered was finding the next party and letting go of the unbelievably empty sadness mixed with confusion about what the hell we're all doing here, which seemed to patiently wait for my sober mind.

I would get angry, too. I would see older people who were doing something I perceived as dumb, and I would bitterly question why the hell they were still alive when such good people died so young. I suppose, when an emotion like grief hits you hard enough, it strips you of everything, including your belief system and your grace. For a person who was always laser-focused on progress, I wanted nothing more than to go backward in time.

When George Bush said that there was an axis of evil threatening our way of life, I believed him. And so did many of my generation. We signed up for the military in droves after the terrorist attacks on September 11, 2001. Tyler was in a foreign country to overthrow their regime because of their alleged possession of weapons of mass destruction. We never did find those weapons, which added to my frustration with life and the God in whom I had believed. I was beginning to skate on thin ice. Adding even a hint of frivolousness to the loss of a life can lead you into a hole so deep you may never get out. You spin endlessly toward the pit of despair, and the pit feels as though it has no bottom. My world was rocked, and nothing made sense.

The hardest part of being inside of a storm is letting go of whatever it is you are holding. The feeling is a lot like getting crushed beneath a big wave: the more you fight, the more the struggle consumes you. Resisting only forces you to use precious oxygen and energy. Similarly, when life is burying you, all that's left is to endure, to ride out the storm, to admit you know nothing and let that be enough for now, to watch the sunrise over and over though you are only in the darkness, and finally to realize that the sun will once again rise on you but that the timeline is not your own and cannot be hurried.

I was lucky enough to have friends and colleagues who knew me before this dip in productivity and character. I was lucky enough to come out on the other side with a career and some key friendships still intact. I say lucky because I did nothing in my grief to deserve good fortune. I was reckless, but somehow, by the grace of God, I came out in a place that allowed me to find my new normal.

Six to seven months down the road, I had a moment where I felt the sun begin to rise. Getting ready to process out of the military, I was home on Christmas leave. One night, sitting around with old friends, smoking a joint, and laughing about whatever stoned people laugh about, I came to the stark realization that if I let the storm win, the last six years were all for nothing. I had no plan, and I was going to be back in my hometown, with little direction and little to show for it other than an attitude that would eventually drive away even the best kinds of people.

Sometimes, when despair lifts and you get a second to be honest with yourself about the road you are on, you should just take it. No great epiphany happened, and I was given no quotable moment. I had no idea what I wanted, but I knew once again that it was time to keep going, in the name of progress if for nothing else. As humans, we come from a lineage of millions of years of survivors, and that just has to mean something.

After the holidays, I went back to my duty station, and I reached out to a mentor for help. I told him that I had always had an interest in being a medic, and he pulled strings to get me into a school for which, by all measures, I was unqualified. I reenlisted, and four months later, I found myself sitting in Fort Bragg, North Carolina, taking on the notoriously difficult Special Operations Combat-Medic course. Suddenly, with people failing all around me, I was back in my element. With the single purpose of passing the class, there was nothing left to do but work hard, endure, and outlast the difficult times. To raise money, Tyler's family had bracelets made that said, "Tough times don't last, tough people do." For ten years, I've been allowing that maxim to guide me and help me make sense of the many despairing pits our lives funnel us into.

Perhaps because of the movies we watch, or maybe just because of childhood wonder, we often want something magical to happen. We want to wake up and have a different or better life, and if that attitude goes too long, we'll end up waiting our entire lives for a date with destiny that is actually at the other end of the work we are avoiding. Magic only happens when you make a conscious decision day in and day out to look for it.

The recipe for magic looks a lot like working hard enough through different endeavors until you find the ones that align with who you are. It's never about what you are doing now, because you are not aware of the future enough to know how what you are doing now will affect you later. You might keep doing what you feel drawn to now because, in three years, you are going to meet the person you'll partner with, which will end up creating the business that thrusts you into financial freedom. Or maybe not. But in any case, you don't know, and you do still have to do something while you're here.

The difference between those who succeed and those who do not is almost never one characteristic or defining attribute other than endurance. I went through a special forces selection program that saw more than a seventy percent attrition rate in my class. I have been an instructor at Basic Underwater Demolition School (BUD/s) SEAL and watched over four thousand students try to be either Navy SEALs or a Special Warfare

Combatant Craft Crewmen (SWCC). In that time, I watched all walks of life come through to try a hand at making it. Olympic athletes, doctors, division one athletes, kids who grew up homeless, and affluent kids all tried their hands at the program.

Out of all of them, the only ones who made it were the ones who got up every morning on little sleep and with sore muscles and were willing to do it all over again the next day. I did notice, however, that people who had experienced a difficult life seemed to have a better chance at making it through. Many really smart and talented people just have not yet seen enough adversity to know that sometimes endurance is a better strategy than talent and you do not need to always know what to do or be the best at what you are doing to keep doing it.

Successful people often look back at particularly difficult times as defining moments in their story. When times grew rough and they were thinking about throwing in the towel, they stuck it out, and soon after, the clouds began to part. If you knew beyond a shadow of a doubt that you would eventually be successful if you just outlasted the hard times, would you be more inclined to persevere? Of course you would, so why don't you start framing things that way. Why don't you commit to the hard times as if they are nothing more than an inevitable part of how you get to where you want to be? Make it a spiritual practice if that helps. When you can see nothing in front of you, the next step might just be enough, but you won't know until you take it.

Chapter 9. You're Never Done

"Don't let fatigue make a coward of you."
–Steve Prefontaine

We will make our share of mistakes along the way. It is possible that we will spend too much time on things that don't matter and miss things that matter immensely. Such is the way with the perpetually intrigued and starving for life. We will have no shortage of difficulties. With that said, if the thought of risk, setbacks, and failures are enough to make us cave and go cowering back to safety and comfort for good, then we will never get further than we are right now. There is no greater shame than missing out on an incredible future because one does not have the correct mindset when dealing with the present.

Can you ask yourself the tough questions and answer honestly? If you can't look all the risk directly in the face and take a step forward anyway, toward the life you really want, then you and I are on different paths. This is not to say we will always rise to the occasion; it is to say that rising is the goal. Every human has to have their non-negotiables in life, and I decided long ago that settling for a mediocre life due to fear of the unknown would always be mine.

I know that the human spirit is capable of more than I know. I've seen an inkling of my own capabilities, and that is enough to keep me coming back to the unknown for a lifetime. A life of learning through discovery will always be my path regardless of how difficult, foreign, or dark that path might look. This is important to acknowledge because many people will say they value growth or freedom or something that speaks to their soul but find they are unwilling to sacrifice what their value demands.

Freedom demands the presence of danger and risk. True growth asks us to leave comfort and keep an open heart no matter how badly the world wants to close it. And if we are the type of people who value freedom and growth and we've found we are cowering from risk and resting on what's comfortable and, further, that our inner state is deteriorating as a result of not living up to who we are here to be, it's important that we find the courage to do the tough thing. Ask yourself right now; what it is you are not doing that your values demand you do? Then be open to whatever arises as that is your path. Finally, work through the resistance keeping you from doing it so you can get on with the part of life that gives you fulfillment.

To be quite honest, I know that given the choice, I wouldn't change anything. The struggle exists for people like me, and people like me were born for the struggle. I just need to get to the other side of the pain, where empowerment and contentment lie, at least until this horizon is defeated and the next one is presented. It's time to lace up the boots and get to work. The job is never done. You're never done. The iterations are endless, so every one presents the potential to grow closer to who you are here to be. Above all, the potential to maximize the only life you are given is endless. The secret that people who die happy know is that if we present all of ourselves to all of our opportunities, life will have our back. If we give ourselves to this life, this life will give itself to us.

In doing so, you will inspire others solely for the fact that you are doing what you love, not just because you are conquering goals and ticking things off your list, but because, when someone is truly in love with the process, it's contagious. Being who you are gives other people permission to be who they are. In that, we see how absurd it is when we are all running around acting like people we are not and doing things that do not set our soul on fire.

And so, you have to go for it. You never know whom you will be inspiring, and you'll never convince me that the world doesn't need more of that. Lots of people are stuck in a life of hell because no one around them has given them permission to leave and they have not yet come to grips with the fact that their life, consciousness, and sovereignty are all the permission that they will ever actually need or have.

Many of the people who give TED talks and motivational speeches and write nonfiction books are often successful because they have a compelling story to tell. Life handed them a particularly difficult situation, and they figured out a way to get through it and thrive. By extrapolating some of the methods they have used and by exploring the details of their triumph in a compelling way, the rest of us can gain a lot.

Inevitably, this will not be the case for all of us. Some of us will have to seek out adversity and go to it. What we'll find is that if we do, it is much more palatable when we are thrust into it. A great life requires that we contend with adversity in a way that allows us to grow, and this is not optional. If we are to find the best life has to offer, we have to be willing to experience some of the most difficult things it has to offer.

A better life is similar to jumping out of an airplane

For all the careening at terminal velocity and the gut-wrenching, inverted circles that might take place, skydiving has, for the most part, proven to be safe. The law of percentages, not to mention a thorough pre-jump checklist, allows even the perpetually grounded humans a feeling of flight while safely drifting back to the ground—uncomfortably shaken up, perhaps, on the edge of fear, for sure, a bit worn out and uncomfortable from a bout of fisticuffs with gravity, but nevertheless returned safely and unchanged, except for the ear-to-ear smile, new transcendence of spirit, and itch to go again, maybe even to go bigger.

Skydiving for the first time can teach us a lot about what goes into creating a great life. You have to find the right combination of being grounded and taking flight. Throw in a little risk while minimizing the downside, and don't fear the first step even if it feels like there's nothing there but air. The best experiences happen when you let go of whatever it is that you might be holding on to. Staying grounded in life requires self-awareness, while jumping into the unknown requires an affinity for adventure and, from time to time, the willingness to stretch your tolerance for risk.

What do you live for? Better yet, what are you willing to die for? Do you know? Who you are, what you like, what your purpose is—these are all of the deep questions that philosophers dedicate their lives to and almost everyone else spends their life avoiding. Asking yourself the difficult questions and answering honestly are the only things that will lead you to a higher state of being, perhaps even to a life that you love, instead of one that you accept.

Most people don't pursue the life they love simply because they don't know what it is they actually love. The universe will drop hints, but if you spend every day entrenched in the mundane, you'll never pick up on them. You have to be willing to unbiasedly explore all the parts of life that don't readily present themselves. Search for alternative conversations outside the mainstream media, in podcasts, books, or any of the various new media sources. By exposing yourself to new ideas, over time, you will learn what you identify with and what is not for you. You may even see that you've been carrying around a story that is not yours for years.

In the end, it will not matter whether you operate your life based on some societal standard set by others. What will matter is whether you can say that you have maximized your one chance at this experience that we call life, whether you can look back on who you were and what you did with contentment.

Devote time to getting to know yourself, and it will pay dividends. When you chase projects, relationships, and careers that don't work out, you will still know who you are and where you stand when the smoke clears, not to mention from where you can begin again. Compare that with the alternative, the all-too-often-used method of tangling your entire character and self-worth in every shiny object that promises relief or attention, and it's easy to see why so many of us are so lost. The risks, the adventures, chasing a dream that no one can see but you, those are the things that make great stories, and that is where growth is found. The caveat is that you have to be certain of who you are to ensure that you don't get lost in the experience. After all, the feeling of flight without returning to the ground loses its allure pretty quickly. Stay grounded in you, and the flight of exploration will be a pleasure rather than a horror show.

Maximizing this human experience requires that we leave no stone unturned. We have to be willing to explore anything and everything we feel drawn to, regardless of whether we have society's approval. We have to be willing to endure when all other options have been stripped away. Paradoxically, we have to be willing to have hard conversations about whether the end justifies the pain we will endure in pursuit of it. And in the event that it does, our endurance should be limitless.

Epilogue. Lukewarm Is Bad for the Soul

*"The years wrinkle our skin, but lack of enthusiasm
wrinkles our soul."*
—Socrates

I once heard that people are likely to remember the first and last thing they read but much of the middle will be lost. In light of that, I would like to leave you with this.

The most dangerous way to live in this world is lukewarm. When the water is only warm enough that it doesn't give you a reason to leave, you'll stay in an environment that doesn't serve you far longer than you should. When life gives you just enough to keep you from being miserable, what it really gives you is just enough to create the space for resentment to form.

Many relationships will satisfy our need for a warm body, but our soul doesn't need a warm body other than our own; our insecurities do. Our soul needs someone that feels like home while simultaneously feeling like our greatest adventure.

Golden handcuffs speak to the mind that believes in scarcity. The ego evolved to cope with a finite world, so it will trick you into believing you have to take a piece of the pie when offered. The soul, on the other hand, is unchained and abundant, so it understands there are virtually unlimited pieces for unlimited people. Due to this, the soul will never accept something it doesn't long for, simply because it is the first or seemingly only thing that is offered. The soul understands that nothing in this world is what it seems. If you accept it despite the nudging of the soul, you'll find yourself having to escape more and more as you grow disconnected from all that you are.

The soul exists below the surface, so the world it sees is deeper than the one you do. The things your soul understands are deeper than the things you understand. On the surface of your life, you'll often feel that everything is fine, while, below the surface, you'll have a sneaking suspicion that something is stirring you to move.

Your soul will push you to get up and search for what else might be, because it knows that this process is where you'll find out what else you could be. It'll nudge you toward things that feel uncomfortable, because, where you see an obstacle, the soul recognizes a path with an opportunity for growth. Where you see what's been broken, it sees where mending will make you stronger.

If you are being pulled to leave a situation that's no longer fully serving you, it's likely that your soul has grown tired of the stagnation and sees a future you cannot. There's something better, bigger, or more worthy of your mettle, and that's the thing your soul has been put here to find. To follow a path you can't fully see is the ultimate act of faith in yourself, and while faith can be a scary way to live your life, the rewards are far greater than the lukewarm purgatory that the smallest parts of you would have you settle for. Happy searching.

Made in the USA
Middletown, DE
20 March 2021